The Eyes of Texas
COOKBOOK

ENJOY
Ron Stone

Happy Cookin!!
Bill Springer

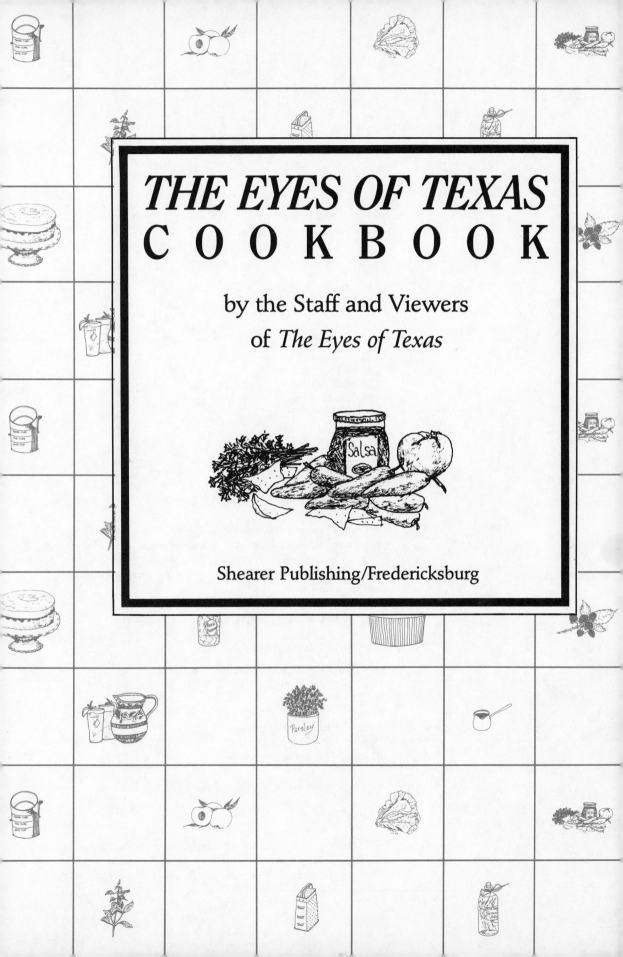

THE EYES OF TEXAS
C O O K B O O K

by the Staff and Viewers
of *The Eyes of Texas*

Shearer Publishing/Fredericksburg

Published in 1987 by
Shearer Publishing
406 Post Oak Road
Fredericksburg, Texas 78624

Copyright © 1987 by KPRC-TV, Houston, Texas

Illustrations copyright © 1987 by Lynn Watt

Photography copyright © 1987 by Don Watt

Library of Congress Cataloging in Publication Data

The Eyes of Texas cookbook.

1. Cookery, American—Southwestern style.
2. Cookery—Texas. I. Eyes of Texas (television program).
TX715.E94   1987   641.59764   87-26547

ISBN 0-940672-43-X (pbk.)

Designed by Barbara Jezek

Manufactured in the United States of America

First Edition

The cover photographs were taken at the Sauer-Beckman
Living History Farm located at the Lyndon B. Johnson State
Historical Park near Stonewall, Texas. The publisher gratefully
acknowledges the farm staff for their assistance.

CONTENTS

INTRODUCTION

When William Least Heat Moon wrote his masterpiece on a journey into America, he named it *Blue Highways* because on most maps the main roads are in red and the back roads are shown in blue. *The Eyes of Texas* has spent eighteen or so years traveling the "blue highways" of Texas. This Houston-based television program rarely goes anywhere you can fly. Sometimes we find ourselves headed for places even difficult to drive to.

Gary James, who has been with the program since its birth, has looked for Brit Bailey's Light and the Marfa Lights; he has been to the International Possum Museum in Rhonesboro; watched 'em make cane syrup at Liberty; and eaten the best and the worst chicken-fried steak in Texas.

Bill Springer, who has put in nine years as a cameraman/reporter for the program, has been to Buck Naked, ridden a train into Moscow, eaten a cowboy breakfast as the sun rose over the Palo Duro Canyon, and snapped beans with storytellers in East Texas.

The program averages four stories a week, so in its lifetime it has presented over three thousand sketches of Texas history or heritage. It has scraped the surface of the unique characters who populate this place that is surely blessed with a variety of folk.

Gary and Bill have watched Texans gather roasting ears, make clabbered milk, and fry up sowbelly and a mess of poke salad. They have had hush puppies in Lufkin, and crumbled cornbread into sweet milk at Post.

Throughout the Hill Country and central Texas they have tasted the fine old foods that came with the European immigrants who walked in to settle this land. To the south they have enjoyed Mexican food as it was meant to be before someone invented neon and freeways.

In all the travels, one constant remained: Texans love to eat. Often as Gary or Bill (or the dozen or so other people who have been *Eyes of Texas* cameramen/reporters) said their good-byes, a copy of a recipe would be thrust into their hands—a recipe that had been handed down, revised, and tried by the women who frequent the all-day-singings and dinners-on-the-grounds, the cake walks and the pie suppers. Early in 1987 we decided to publish those recipes and made appeals for others. This book is the result.

As usual, reaching out to the people paid extra dividends. Many of the recipes included notes. Laura Phipps of Mineral Wells sent us her best fish recipe learned from long-ago summers at Rollover Pass, where Papaw caught the fish and the family fried 'em.

Then there was Pearl Monaghan who once lived on the famous La Gloria ranch, where her husband was the foreman. She shared her many ways of preparing prickly pear. She is eighty-two now and still going strong, so there must be something to eating prickly pears.

Ben Scholl, who lives in Tomball, sent us a recipe for Honey Cookies. It was handed down from his great-grandparents, who operated a steam cotton gin in Washington County. They did not have much money, says Scholl, but there was an abundance of bees and native pecans; so today we can enjoy what August and Caroline Weiss's resourcefulness left us.

This is homey stuff: you won't lose weight eating this food. Gary James says you can always tell a good chicken-fried steak cafe by whether or not you can smell the hot grease when you open the car door in the parking lot. And one of the great truths I have learned as a naturalized Texan is that you should never trust anyone who doesn't like fried okra.

Open this book and start cooking. When you eat, smile or laugh if you want, but enjoy, and say a little prayer of thanks that God let you be a Texan.

Ron Stone
Houston
May 1987

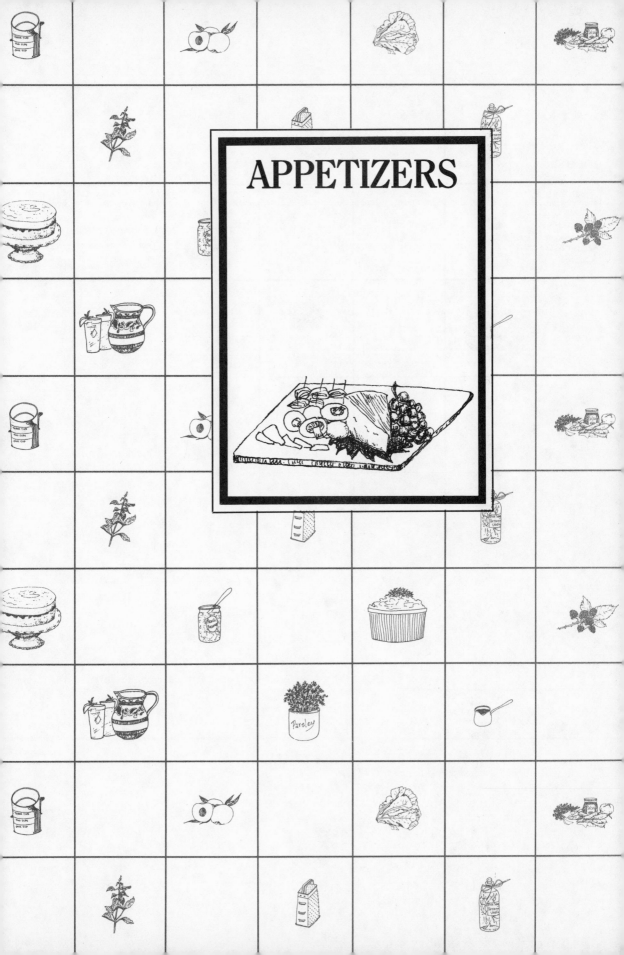

APPETIZERS

TEXAS GARDEN DIP

2 tomatoes, chopped
4 green onions, chopped
1 4-ounce can chopped green chilies
1 2¼-ounce can chopped black olives
3 tablespoons salad oil
2 tablespoons vinegar
1 teaspoon garlic powder
Salt and pepper

Variation:
Spread an 8-ounce package of cream cheese on a tray and top with this dip.

Mix tomatoes, onion, chilies (drained) and olives (drained) with oil, vinegar and garlic powder in bowl. Salt and pepper to taste. Serve with tortilla chips as a delicious appetizer.
Better if made the night before.
A dash or two of picante sauce makes this even better.

Donnette Connally
Texas City, Texas

TEXAS BEAN DIP

Heat together:
1 can refried beans with chorizo
1 stick butter

Add:
½ onion, finely chopped
1 to 2 jalapeños (or to taste)
½ pound sharp cheddar cheese, grated
½ teaspoon garlic juice

Heat to boiling. Serve with corn chips.

Mary V. Bogles
El Paso, Texas

GUACAMOLE DIP

6 ripe avocados, mashed
2 8-ounce packages cream cheese, softened
3 tablespoons lemon juice
3 tablespoons picante sauce
1–2 tablespoons jalapeño green sauce
Salt and pepper

Mix avocados and cream cheese well. Add other ingredients. Adjust seasonings to taste. Mix well. Serve with chips. Keep refrigerated.

Debbie Henderson
Houston, Texas

PINK HAM DIP

1 8-ounce package cream cheese
½ cup mayonnaise
2 tablespoons ketchup
1 3-inch section of celery stalk
2 ounces cooked ham, cut in pieces
2 tablespoons fresh parsley leaves, chopped
Salt
8 to 10 pitted olives

Process all ingredients except olives with metal blade in food processor until smooth, about 15 seconds. Add olives. Process until olives are finely chopped in mixture. Serve chilled with your favorite crackers or chips.

Margaret R. Bullock
Lufkin, Texas

TRUE-GRIT TEXAS TRASH

1 box Corn Chex
1 box Rice Chex
1 box Bran Chex
1 box Wheat Chex
1 large bag thin pretzels
1 large bag regular Fritos
1 box Cheerios
2 pounds roasted peanuts

Heat the following ingredients in a large pot:
1 stick margarine
¾ cup bacon drippings
½ cup Worcestershire sauce
1 whole small bottle Tabasco
2 tablespoons garlic salt

Heat and simmer 3 minutes. Mix in slowly with ingredients above. Bake on cookie sheets in slow oven (250°) for 1 hour. Stir often while baking. Makes a huge bag of snacks for holidays. Store air-tight.

Kathy Vignone
Santa Fe, Texas

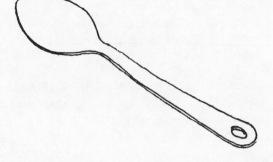

ARMADILLO EGGS

½ pound Monterey jack cheese
½ pound cheddar cheese
½ pound bulk hot sausage
1½ cups Bisquick mix
15 to 20 medium to large canned jalapeño peppers
1 egg
1 package Shake 'n Bake for pork

Grate cheese (both kinds) and mix together, then divide in half. Mix together half of the grated cheese, the raw sausage and the Bisquick mix. Knead until stiff dough is formed. Set aside. Slit jalapeño peppers and remove seeds. Do not rinse. Stuff each pepper with remaining cheese. Pinch pepper together to seal. Now pinch off a bit of dough mixture and pat into a pancake approximately ¼-inch thick. Place stuffed pepper in middle and roll in hand to form egg shape. Roll each ball in beaten egg and then in Shake 'n Bake mixture. Bake at 325° for 20 minutes. These may be frozen and baked later.

Kathy Vignone
Santa Fe, Texas

TEXAS CHEESE SQUARES

1 2¼-ounce can ripe olives, sliced
1 4-ounce can green chilies, chopped
1 2-ounce jar pimientos, diced (optional)
½ pound sharp cheddar cheese, grated
½ pound Monterey jack cheese, grated
1 cup biscuit mix
1 cup milk
4 large eggs

Grease a square casserole, then layer with olives, green chilies, and pimientos (if used). Cover with cheddar cheese, then layer with Monterey jack cheese. Mix biscuit mix, milk, and eggs well. Pour evenly over layers. Bake at 375° until set and golden brown. Cool slightly, then cut into small squares. Good hot or cold, and freezes well.

Vera Lightsey
Houston, Texas

BEST-EVER CHEESE STRAWS

2 sticks butter
2⅔ cups flour
4 cups grated sharp cheddar cheese
1½ teaspoons cayenne pepper

Mix all ingredients thoroughly in mixer or with pastry cutter. Using the star tube, put the mixture through cookie press onto cookie sheet. Bake 20 minutes at 300°. Serve hot or cold.

Lanelle Jolly
Texas City, Texas

HALLELUJAH CHEESE BALL

1 pound grated sharp cheddar cheese
1 8-ounce package cream cheese
2 tablespoons parsley flakes
¼ cup mayonnaise
1 teaspoon garlic powder or 2 cloves fresh garlic
1 12-ounce can sliced jalapeños, drained
Chopped pecans

Place all ingredients in food processor and mix just until blended. Refrigerate. Make a large ball and roll in lots of chopped pecans. Serve with crackers or bread.

Yvonne L. Treacy
Houston, Texas

BIG-CHEESE OLIVES

1 8-ounce package cream cheese
1 3-ounce package cream cheese
1 teaspoon salad dressing
1½ teaspoons horseradish (or to taste)
1 large bottle of large stuffed olives (about 20)
2 or more cups pecans, chopped fine

Put cream cheese out to soften. Using mixer, cream it with the salad dressing and horseradish. Using hands, shape cream cheese mixture around each olive. (Mixture may need to be slightly refrigerated to work with.) Then roll this in chopped pecans. Put these in refrigerator overnight. Then cut lengthwise to serve. These are really worth the effort at Christmas.

Annie Belle Gibbs
Montgomery, Texas

SPINACH BALLS

2 10-ounce packages frozen chopped spinach
1 box Stove Top chicken-flavored stuffing mix, uncooked
6 eggs
1 cup grated Parmesan cheese
¾ cup butter or margarine, softened
Salt and pepper

Cook spinach as directed and drain well. In a medium bowl, mix all ingredients well. Refrigerate 30 minutes. Make 1-inch-round balls. Place on cookie sheet and put in freezer. When frozen, remove from cookie sheet and store in plastic bags that seal well. Keep frozen until ready to bake. Bake on cookie sheet from 10 to 15 minutes at 350°. Be careful not to brown too much.

Gladys Holmes
Houston, Texas

JALAPEÑO COCKTAIL PIE

½ cup chopped and seeded jalapeño peppers
1 pound sharp cheddar cheese, grated
6 eggs, well beaten

Lightly grease an 8- or 9-inch square pan. Put in ingredients in order given and bake for 30 minutes at 350°. Cool and cut into 1-inch squares and serve with toothpicks.

Judy Fallin
Conroe, Texas

CHERRY TOMATOES WITH SMOKED OYSTERS

Cherry tomatoes
Canned smoked oysters

Wash tomatoes (do not remove stems). Cut down through each tomato to within ½ inch of base. Spread apart just enough to slip in a canned smoked oyster. Serve at room temperature or slightly chilled.

Note: A 3-ounce can usually contains about 40 tiny oysters.

Mrs. Joe Morecraft, Jr.
Texas City, Texas

JACKIE'S SMOKED SALMON BALL (1987)

1 1-pound can or 2 cups salmon
1 8-ounce package cream cheese, softened
1 tablespoon lemon juice
2 teaspoons grated onion
1 teaspoon prepared horseradish
¼ teaspoon salt
¼ teaspoon liquid smoke
Minced parsley
Chopped pecans

Drain and flake salmon; remove skin and bones. Combine with all ingredients. Mix well. Chill several hours. Roll into ball. Roll in minced parsley and chopped pecans. Serve chilled with crackers or fresh vegetable sticks.

Jackie Vanway
Missouri City, Texas

CRABMEAT-BACON ROLLS

¼ cup tomato juice
1 well-beaten egg
1 7½-ounce can (1 cup) crabmeat, flaked and cartilage
   removed
½ cup fine dry bread crumbs
1 tablespoon chopped parsley
1 tablespoon lemon juice
¼ teaspoon salt
¼ teaspoon Worcestershire sauce
Dash pepper
9 slices bacon, cut in half

Mix tomato juice and egg. Add crab, bread crumbs, parsley, lemon juice, salt, Worcestershire sauce and pepper; mix thoroughly. Roll into 18 fingers, each about 2 inches long. Wrap each roll spiral fashion with ½ slice of bacon; fasten with a toothpick. Broil 5 inches from heat about 10 minutes, turning often to brown evenly. Serve hot.

Gladys M. Lancon
Taylor Lake Village, Texas

CRAB BALL

1 7½-ounce can crabmeat
1 8-ounce package cream cheese, softened
2 teaspoons chopped chives
¼ teaspoon garlic powder
½ teaspoon salt
½ cup finely chopped pecans

Drain crabmeat. Blend softened cream cheese, chives, garlic powder and salt. Fold in crabmeat. Shape into a ball and roll in pecans. Chill overnight. Serve with assorted crackers or chips.

Margaret Nelson
Baytown, Texas

CAVIAR CROWN

3 8-ounce packages cream cheese, softened
3 tablespoons lemon juice
6 tablespoons chopped green onions
1½ teaspoons Worcestershire sauce
½ teaspoon garlic juice
6 drops Tabasco
2 4-ounce jars black caviar
Lemon wedges
Parsley sprigs

Combine first 6 ingredients; beat on medium speed of electric mixer until smooth and fluffy. Place in 8-inch spring-form pan. Refrigerate.

Spoon caviar over tops and sides of cheese circle after spring form has been removed. Garnish with lemon wedges and parsley sprigs. Serve with toast points or thin crackers.

Wilma Bruyere
Houston, Texas

SHRIMP BUTTER

8-ounce package cream cheese
1 stick butter
1 teaspoon garlic salt
1 tablespoon finely chopped green onion tops
1 teaspoon lemon juice
1 cup small shrimp, boiled and shelled

Soften the cream cheese and butter. Combine with the garlic salt, green onion tops, lemon juice and shrimp. Refrigerate. Serve with crackers.

Rita Parker
Houston, Texas

CEVICHE

1 pound fish fillets, finely chopped
1 to 2 cups lime juice (freshly squeezed only)
½ onion, finely chopped
1 to 2 cloves garlic, minced or pressed
1 small bunch cilantro, chopped

Mix ingredients in a plastic or ceramic bowl. Make sure there is enough lime juice to completely cover the mixture. Let the mixture sit covered in the refrigerator for a couple of hours until fish changes color from pink to white. It is even better if left overnight.

Add 1 handful of chopped cilantro before serving. Optional garnishes include chopped avocados and/or tomatoes. Serve with corn tortillas.

Bob Butler
Bastrop, Texas

CRUNCHY CHICKEN BALLS

2 5-ounce cans chunk chicken
1 cup fine dry bread crumbs
¾ cup milk
⅓ cup mayonnaise
1 egg, slightly beaten
¼ cup finely chopped parsley
¼ cup chopped onion
¼ cup chopped walnuts
1 tablespoon prepared mustard
1 teaspoon poultry seasoning
Corn-flake crumbs

In a bowl, mix thoroughly all ingredients except corn-flake crumbs. Shape into small balls, about 1 inch in diameter. Roll in corn-flake crumbs. Arrange in greased shallow baking dish. Bake at 450° for 10 minutes, or until brown. Makes about 4 dozen. Variation: Proceed as above except fry balls in deep hot fat at 375° for 5 minutes or until golden brown.

Mrs. J. W. Thornton
Dickinson, Texas

BEVERAGES

CAFE DE OLLA

1 quart water
½ cup fine-grind coffee
1 stick cinnamon
Piloncillo or dark brown sugar to taste

In a pot (use an earthenware pot, if available), mix water, coffee and cinnamon. Boil 3 to 4 minutes. Stir and strain into mugs. Sweeten with the *piloncillo*. (*Piloncillo* is a cone of dark brown unrefined sugar used as a sweetener in Mexico.)

Mary Ellen Ledesma
Bertram, Texas

WASSAIL

½ gallon apple cider
2 cups canned orange juice (not concentrated)
2 cups canned pineapple juice
½ cup reconstituted lemon juice
1 stick cinnamon
1 teaspoon whole cloves
½ cup sugar

Bring all ingredients to a boil and serve.

Mildred P. Seiler
Johnson City, Texas

EGGNOG

12 eggs, separated
1 cup sugar
1 pint whiskey (2 cups)
½ cup sugar
1 quart milk
Whipped cream
Nutmeg

Beat egg yolks and 1 cup sugar until lemon-colored. Blend in whiskey, slowly. Beat whites until fluffy, but not dry, then add ½ cup sugar to whites, mixing well.

Blend whiskey mixture slowly into beaten egg whites. Add milk when ready to serve. Spoon on whipped cream and a dash of nutmeg.

Bobbie Dykes
Bay City, Texas

MOCK CHAMPAGNE

1 cup unsweetened apple juice
¼ cup grape juice
3 cups 7-Up, Sprite or Slice

Mix all ingredients. Pour over ice in tall glasses.
   Variation: Mix fruit juices and freeze. When ready to serve, chip frozen juices into icy chunks and pour soda over.

Odalee Martin
Willis, Texas

PINK LADY PUNCH

1½ cups sugar
4 cups cranberry juice
4 cups pineapple juice
2 quarts ginger ale, chilled

Dissolve sugar in cranberry juice. Add remaining ingredients and chill.

Betty Lou Warren
Texas City, Texas

GOLDEN SHERBET PUNCH

2 cups sugar
1½ cups fresh mint leaves
2 cups boiling water
¾ cup lemon juice
1 12-ounce can apricot nectar, chilled
1 6-ounce can frozen limeade concentrate
1 6-ounce can frozen orange juice concentrate
1 6-ounce can frozen pineapple juice concentrate
2 large bottles ginger ale, chilled
1 quart lemon sherbet
Fresh mint sprigs for garnish

Combine sugar, mint and boiling water; stir to dissolve sugar. Chill. Strain into chilled punch bowl; add lemon juice, apricot nectar and concentrates. Pour ginger ale down side of bowl. Top with scoops of sherbet. Trim with fresh mint. Serves 20 to 25.
   Variation: Add vodka, if desired.

Karen R. Thompson
Austin, Texas

PARTY TIME PUNCH

1 12-ounce can frozen citrus drink concentrate
4 12-ounce cans water
1 12-ounce can ginger ale
1 small lemon, sliced, then halved
1 small apple, sliced into wedges

Combine all ingredients and refrigerate 2 hours before serving. Makes approximately 2 quarts.

Jo Adele Hughes
Houston, Texas

SHERBET PUNCH

3 quarts ginger ale
1 gallon sherbet, orange or lime

Chill ginger ale. Chill punch bowl with ice cubes and discard ice. About 30 minutes before party, pour chilled ginger ale into punch bowl. Add sherbet with ice cream scoop. Let melt slightly. Serve with little bits of sherbet in each cup.

Lenee MacDonald
Romayor, Texas

INSTANT SPICED TEA

2 cups instant orange drink
½ cup instant tea
½ cup sugar
1 package lemonade mix
1 teaspoon cinnamon
1 teaspoon nutmeg

Mix ingredients in order given. Stir well. Store in jars with lids. Makes about 3 cups mix.
   To use, add 1 teaspoon to 1 tablespoon of spiced tea mix to a cup of hot water.

Lenee Macdonald
Romayor, Texas

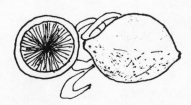

NOTES:

SOUPS

GRANDMA'S VEGETABLE BEEF SOUP

1 pound stew meat
¼ cup cooking oil
6 cups water
1 can tomatoes, chopped
1 can beef broth
½ teaspoon pepper
1 tablespoon chili powder
Few drops Tabasco sauce
1 tablespoon vinegar
1 can tomato sauce
1 small can V-8 juice
1 teaspoon salt
2 teaspoons garlic powder
1 tablespoon Worcestershire sauce
2 tablespoons sugar

1 onion, or bunch of green onions
½ bell pepper
½ cup celery leaves
¾ stick margarine
3 carrots
20 ounces frozen mixed vegetables
2 tablespoons parsley
5 medium potatoes
1 tablespoon Italian herbs
1 tablespoon basil

Cut fat off of meat and cut into small bite-size pieces. Cook in oil until lightly browned. Add water and all ingredients in first section. Cook 30 minutes. While this is cooking on low to medium heat, chop onion, bell pepper and celery, and cook on low heat in ¾ stick of margarine about 15 minutes, then add to meat mixture. Cut carrots into small bite-size pieces. Add carrots, frozen vegetables and parsley to meat. Cook 25 more minutes. Cut potatoes into small bite-size pieces. Add potatoes, herbs and basil to meat mixture and cook 20 more minutes. Test vegetables to be sure they are done.

Don and Miriam Kimball
Alvin, Texas

OXTAIL SOUP

Oxtails
Seasoned salt
1 package Knorr Oxtail Soup mix
1 package Knorr Onion Soup mix
1 package frozen soup vegetables

Cook oxtails in small amount of water, seasoning with a small amount of seasoned salt. Cook until tender. Mix both soup mixes in water called for on packages until well blended; add to oxtails along with frozen vegetables. Cook on low heat until done. You can add ½ cup of pasta or barley to give soup more body.

Mary O. Farris
Houston, Texas

DAD'S MAIL-ORDER VEGETABLE SOUP

"When I first made this soup, I had to call my Dad for pointers. He always put everything but the kitchen sink in his soup. He gave me some tips, but with one stipulation . . . I had to send him some before I could serve it to anyone. Of course, I did—he's my Dad! I shipped him a large Ziploc bag, Federal Express Next-Day-Air."

3 cans beef bouillon
6 cups water
3 tablespoons Worcestershire sauce
2 tablespoons oregano
½ tablespoon sage
1 bay leaf (remove before eating)
2½ tablespoons black pepper
1½ tablespoons basil
1 teaspoon salt
1½ pounds stew beef (1- to 2-inch cubes)
1 pound new potatoes, peeled
1 pound carrots, peeled (sliced ½-inch round)
1 pound fresh green beans, broken in 1-inch pieces
1 small turnip, diced
2 ears yellow corn (slice corn off cob)
4 medium tomatoes, peeled and cubed
2 small zucchini, diced
2 medium okra, sliced
1 stalk celery, chopped
3 small yellow squash, diced

In a 12-quart stockpot bring bouillon and water to a boil. Lower heat. Put in all seasonings. In separate pan, brown meat on all sides. Put meat with all juices into stock. Raise heat on stock to medium for 2 hours. Simmer for 2 more hours. Test meat every hour. When meat is tender, but not falling apart, cut potatoes into 2-inch cubes and put into stock along with carrots, green beans, turnip and corn. Cook on medium for ½ hour. Stir often. Put in remaining vegetables, cook for another ½ hour. Test after 15 minutes; stir. Cook until all vegetables are tender, with only a slight crunch. Eat when hungry. You can omit the beef if you wish.

Elizabeth C. Roth
Houston, Texas

MULLIGA-TAWNY SOUP

½ cup onion, finely chopped
3 tablespoons butter
2½ tablespoons flour
2 tablespoons curry powder
1 quart chicken broth, heated
1 pint half-and-half
Salt and pepper
1 cup chicken, cooked and cut in thin slices
1 raw, tart apple, peeled and finely chopped
Chopped parsley

In a large saucepan, sauté onion in butter. Stir in flour and curry powder and cook about 2 minutes. Gradually stir in heated broth. Stir constantly until mixture thickens and is smooth. Stir in half-and-half. Season to taste with salt and pepper. Add chicken slices and apple 10 minutes before serving. May garnish with chopped fresh parsley.

Wilda Deas
Houston, Texas

FLYING AWAY SOUP

4 cloves garlic, minced
2 large onions, sliced
1 pound carrots, sliced
1 celery stalk sliced with tops
4 ears of corn, quartered
20 chicken wings, use whole or sectioned, discarding tips
1 small package frozen baby peas
Assorted pasta or substitute potatoes, about 3 medium, cut up

Bring to simmer about 3 quarts water in soup pot. Drop in garlic, onions, carrots, celery and corn. When water is hot again, drop in chicken wings. After chicken wings are done, turn off heat, drop in baby peas and pasta. Salt and pepper to taste. Let sit about 15 minutes before serving.

Mary Ellen Ledesma
Bertram, Texas

CHICKEN NOODLE SOUP

1 large fryer (3½ to 4 pounds)
2 large onions, sliced
4 to 5 stalks celery, cut up
Salt to taste
Black pepper to taste
1 clove garlic
⅓ teaspoon saffron (optional)
6 to 8 whole black peppercorns
1 pound noodles

Put all the ingredients in a large pot except noodles. Add water to cover. Cook until chicken is tender.

Remove chicken, debone and dice. Strain broth. Return diced chicken to broth and bring to a boil. Add noodles, and cook until noodles are soft.

Virginia Helweg
Shiner, Texas

"Chicken noodle soup is good therapy for everything from homesickness to a broken heart."

ROY'S STEAK SOUP

1 to 1½ pounds chuck roast
3 tablespoons oil
3 tablespoons flour
2 tablespoons bell pepper, diced
2 tablespoons white shallots
2 tablespoons white onions
1 can beef broth
2 or 3 cans chicken broth
½ teaspoons salt
¼ teaspoon cumin
¼ teaspoon dried cilantro (or fresh to taste)
¼ teaspoon thyme
¼ teaspoon oregano
2 bay leaves
1 tablespoon parsley
6 drops hot pepper sauce

Remove all fat, skin membranes, tendons, etc., from meat. Cut into ¼-inch cubes. Braise meat in hot oil. Put aside. Make a roux with oil and flour. Sauté vegetables in roux. Add broth and vegetables. Add all seasonings except parsley and hot sauce. Bring to simmer over low fire. Taste to adjust seasonings. Add parsley and hot sauce and continue to simmer for 1½ to 2 hours until meat melts in your mouth. Remove bay leaves before serving.

Roy D. Plaisance
Angleton, Texas

CALDO

1½ pounds round steak, trimmed and cubed
Beef broth or 2 beef bouillon cubes and water to make 3 pints
3 onions, chopped
2 or 3 cloves garlic, chopped
1 4-ounce can green chilies, chopped
3 or 4 peeled tomatoes, or a 16-ounce can with liquid,
   chopped
3 or 4 potatoes, cut up in medium cubes
Salt
¼ teaspoon cumin
Pepper
1 teaspoon oregano

Brown meat with fat trimmings. Add beef broth; simmer covered 1 hour. Take out trimmings and add remaining ingredients. Cook covered several hours on medium to low heat. This Mexican soup should be served with warm flour tortillas.

Mrs. Michael Collier
Missouri City, Texas

SEAFOOD CHOWDER

3 cups diced potatoes
1 cup diced carrots
½ cup minced celery
½ cup minced onion
1 clove garlic, minced
1 teaspoon salt
1 teaspoon pepper
1 bay leaf
½ teaspoon Italian seasoning
Water
3 cups milk
1 cup half-and-half
¼ cup butter
2 8-ounce cans minced clams, undrained
1 quart oysters, drained
¾ pound shrimp, cooked and peeled
½ pound crabmeat

In a saucepan, combine potatoes, carrots, celery, onion, garlic and seasonings. Add water to cover. Bring to a boil, reduce heat and simmer until very tender, about 20 minutes. Remove bay leaf. With an electric mixer or blender, blend vegetables with cooking liquid until smooth. Return to saucepan; add remaining ingredients. Simmer until steaming hot. Do not boil. If thicker soup is desired, thicken with cornstarch. Can be frozen. Serves 8–10.

Fran Payton
The Woodlands, Texas

BORSCHT

2 cups shredded beets
1 cup chopped carrots
1 cup chopped onion
1 tablespoon butter
2 cups beef stock or consommé
1 cup shredded cabbage
1 tablespoon lemon juice
½ cup thick sour cream

Cook beets, carrots and onion for 20 minutes in boiling salted water to cover. Add butter, stock and cabbage; cook 15 minutes. Add lemon juice; pour into bowls. Top with a bit of sour cream. Makes 6 servings.

Bernice Murphy
Hobbs, New Mexico

CREAM OF BROCCOLI SOUP

¼ cup minced onion
¼ cup chopped celery
¼ cup butter
1 bunch broccoli, cooked and chopped
⅓ cup flour
4 cups chicken broth
2 cups heavy cream
Salt and pepper

Sauté onion and celery in butter until tender. Puree half of the broccoli in blender. Add flour and broth to onion and celery in pot. Stir well to mix. Boil 1 minute. Add broccoli and cream. Heat over low heat to serving temperature. Season to taste with salt and pepper. Serve with crackers or croutons.

Lanelle Jolly
Texas City, Texas

FRESH CORN CHOWDER

2 thick slices bacon, chopped
1 onion
2 cups cubed potatoes
3¼ cups boiling water
2 cups fresh cut corn, or canned corn
1 teaspoon salt
⅛ teaspoon pepper
1¾ cups evaporated milk
1 tablespoon butter
1 tablespoon flour

Cook chopped bacon in soup kettle until crisp. Add onion and sauté until transparent. Add potatoes and water and simmer until potatoes are tender. Add corn and seasonings. Mix well and add milk. Melt butter and blend in flour thoroughly, then add slowly to soup, stirring until slightly thickened. Serve piping hot.

Jane Luttrell
Pasadena, Texas

CHEESE SOUP

½ to 1 chopped onion
1 cup carrots
1 cup chopped celery
2 cans cream of chicken soup
6 cans water
1 can Rotel tomatoes
¼ teaspoon white pepper
1 teaspoon salt
1 cup butter or margarine
1 cup flour
2 cups milk
2 pounds cheese, cubed

Chop or blend onion, carrots and celery (may do in blender or food processor). Combine soup, water, onion, carrots and celery. Boil until vegetables are done. Blend Rotel tomatoes and add to cooked soup. Add pepper and salt. Melt butter. Add flour and then milk (as for gravy), making a white sauce. Slowly add cheese to white sauce until all cheese is melted. Stir constantly and keep on low heat. Add cheese mix to soup mix. It is ready to eat. Freezes well.

Jim D. Parker
Pasadena, Texas

BEER-CHEESE SOUP

Cook for 5 minutes the following:
½ cup onion, finely diced
½ cup celery, finely diced
½ cup carrots, finely diced
3 tablespoons margarine

Stir into the above and cook until smooth, approximately 2 minutes:
3 tablespoons flour
1 tablespoon cornstarch

Over low heat, add the following in order, stirring continuously:
2 cups milk
½ can beer
2 cups chicken broth
4 teaspoons Worcestershire sauce
Ground cayenne and seasoned salt to taste
2 pounds Velveeta cheese, cubed

Stir until cheese melts and soup is hot.

Gayle Yoder
Seabrook, Texas

ONION SOUP

6 large onions
3 cloves garlic
12 tablespoons butter
9 tablespoons flour
10 cups chicken stock (may use canned)
2 cups dry white wine
Salt and freshly ground black pepper to taste
Swiss cheese, grated (optional)

Peel and chop the onions very fine. Mince the garlic cloves. Heat the butter in a saucepan, add the onions and garlic, stirring slowly over medium heat until the onion is golden but not browned. Blend in the flour and stir for 3 minutes. Add the chicken stock all at once. Raise the heat slightly and stir the soup rapidly until it comes to a boil. Add the wine and simmer the soup for 20 minutes, stirring from time to time. Serve immediately with grated Swiss cheese if desired. Freezes wonderfully.

Wilma Bruyere
Houston, Texas

FRENCH ONION SOUP

⅓ cup margarine
4 cups sliced onion
3 10½-ounce cans condensed beef broth
2 cups water
½ teaspoon salt
Dash pepper
6 to 8 slices French bread, toasted
1 cup freshly grated Parmesan cheese

Melt margarine in a large heavy saucepan. Add onion and sauté until golden brown. Stir in condensed beef broth, water, salt and pepper. Bring to a boil; cover, reduce heat and let simmer 25 minutes. To serve, place soup in individual ovenproof soup bowls or tureen. Top with bread slices and grated cheese. Bake at 400° about 5 minutes or until cheese is melted. (Or melt cheese by placing in a microwave a few seconds.) Makes 6 to 8 servings.

Doris Dyson
Houston, Texas

CREAM OF POTATO SOUP SUPREME

Cut up the following and put in a large covered pot to simmer until the carrots are done, about 25 minutes:
2 cups water
2 large carrots
2 ribs celery
4 large potatoes
Salt and pepper
2 bunches green onions
1 medium onion
½ pound ham (or turkey ham)

After the vegetables are done, add:
1 8-ounce jar of Cheez Whiz (mild jalapeño is very good) or
8-ounce package of Velveeta

Stir until cheese is melted. Remove from heat and add small container of sour cream. If you desire thinner soup, add water or milk to get the desired consistency.

Marguerite K. Turner
Houston, Texas

SPINACH SOUP

1 package frozen spinach
1 can chicken broth
Half-and-half or cream
¼ teaspoon nutmeg
½ teaspoon salt
Pepper
2 tablespoons chopped onion
2 tablespoons butter
1 tablespoon chopped parsley

Cook spinach in some of the broth. Whirl in blender. Add rest of chicken broth and cream, and heat. Add seasonings. Cook onion in butter, puree in blender and add to soup. Add parsley.

Crispina Babbitt
Austin, Texas

SPINACH SOUP, HOUSTON STYLE

1 small package frozen spinach
2 tablespoons butter
2 tablespoons fresh chopped yellow onion
1 teaspoon lemon juice
1½ teaspoons chicken bouillon granules
Pinch black pepper
1 cup milk
1 cup whipping cream or heavy cream
¼ teaspoon fresh grated nutmeg
Grated Parmesan cheese

Cook spinach until almost done and do not salt or season. Drain and put in the blender with butter, onion, lemon juice, chicken granules and pepper. Blend all of the above until puree stage, then pour back in the pot that you cooked the spinach in. Then clean all the spinach out of the blender with the milk. Pour milk into the pot with the soup mixture. Add the whipping cream and nutmeg. Heat almost to boiling point and put in serving bowls. Garnish center of each bowl of soup with Parmesan cheese.

Corinne Flukinger
Houston, Texas

BEAN SOUP

1 cup large lima beans (butter beans)
1 cup small white (navy) beans
2 quarts water
1 smoked ham hock
1 onion, chopped
1 tablespoon sugar
Salt and pepper

Put all ingredients in large soup pot and bring to a boil. Take off heat for 30 minutes. Put back on medium heat and simmer till beans are soft (2 to 3 hours), adding water as necessary. When done, remove about a cup of beans and liquid, puree in blender or food processor, and add back to soup to thicken.

Ann Reddehase
Houston, Texas

UNCLE JOE'S BEAN SOUP

2 pounds pinto beans
2 pounds bacon ends
1 stalk celery
1 bunch green onions
3 or 4 yellow onions
2 or 3 bell peppers
3 or 4 jalapeño peppers
3 or 4 cloves garlic
2 cans stewed tomatoes
Cilantro to taste
1 teaspoon paprika
2 tablespoons poultry seasoning
Salt to taste
1 cup wine (optional)

Soak beans overnight. Cut up bacon ends, celery, onions, peppers, garlic and tomatoes. Pour water off the beans and put them in a 2- or 3-gallon pot. Add garlic and boil in water about 2 inches over beans. While the beans are boiling, fry the bacon (not crisp) in at least a 6-quart saucepan. Add tomatoes, celery, green peppers, onions, jalapeños, and spices. Let stew for about 30 minutes; then pour in with beans. Turn back to simmer for at least 2 hours. Add salt to taste and 1 cup wine, and let simmer for at least 30 minutes to 1 hour. Soup is also good without wine, and it freezes well.

Cynthia Wendel
Danbury, Texas

RED LENTIL SOUP CARIBE

2 cups red lentils
7 cups water
4 chicken bouillon cubes
½ cup chopped onion
1 large potato, diced
2 cups diced carrots
1 tablespoon celery seed
1 tablespoon curry powder
1½ tablespoons chile caribe
1 bay leaf
2 cloves garlic

"Here it is. Sam Richardson's World Famous Red Lentil Soup *Caribe!* Who said it was World Famous? Who said it wasn't?

"Red lentils are a cousin to regular lentils, split peas and yellow peas, but red lentils are much lighter and cook quicker. They'll fluff up to a nice golden texture in about thirty minutes.

"*Chile caribe* is just dried red pepper flakes. Any kind of dried peppers can be used —New Mexico reds, *chiles ancho,* etc."

Wash lentils. Put lentils in a pot with water and bouillon cubes and bring to a boil. Then remove from heat and set aside while you chop up onion, potato and carrots. Add vegetables and all spices to the pot and bring back to the boil. Lower heat and cook for about an hour.

Sam Richardson
Austin, Texas

BLACK BEAN SOUP

1 pound black beans
Ham bone or cubed ham bits
1 cup chopped celery
1 cup chopped carrots
½ cup chopped onion
1 12-ounce can tomato paste
2 bay leaves
2 cloves garlic, finely minced
Salt and pepper

Soak beans overnight in water. Discard water and add fresh water to cover. Simmer beans and ham 1½ to 2 hours. Add vegetables and seasonings. Cook 1½ to 2 more hours. Just before serving, cut ham from the ham hock or bone and return it to the soup.

Elizabeth Sadler
Houston, Texas

BEAN-AND-SAUSAGE SOUP

2 onions, chopped
6 cloves garlic, chopped
6 teaspoons cooking oil
1 pound smoked sausage, sliced ¼-inch thick
4 cans beef broth
1 8-ounce can tomato sauce
½ teaspoon black pepper
1 can kidney beans, undrained
1 head green cabbage, cored and shredded
12 small new potatoes, quartered
¼ cup vinegar
Salt

Sauté onion and garlic in oil. Add sausage. Brown slightly. Add remaining ingredients. Bring to a boil. Stir well. Reduce heat. Cover and simmer 1 hour. Soup is even better the second day.

Lanelle Jolly
Texas City, Texas

CHILLED CUCUMBER SOUP

4 cups buttermilk
2 cups sour cream
3 tablespoons fresh parsley, chopped
1 teaspoon salt
2 cucumbers, peeled, chopped, seeds removed
1 small white onion, chopped
Dash Tabasco sauce
1 small cucumber, unpeeled and chopped

Place all ingredients in a blender except the small cucumber, and blend until smooth. Do this in batches. Serve in chilled bowls and garnish with unpeeled cucumber.

Wilma Bruyere
Houston, Texas

LEMON SOUP

6 cups chicken broth
¼ cup long grain rice
1 teaspoon salt
3 eggs
¼ cup fresh lemon juice
1 lemon, sliced thick for garnish

Combine broth, rice and salt, and bring to a boil. Reduce heat, cover and simmer for about 15 minutes, until rice is done. Remove from heat. In a bowl beat eggs until fluffy and pale yellow. Add lemon juice. Slowly stir 2 cups hot broth into egg mixture. Return to pan with rest of hot broth and whisk together until slightly thickened. Cool to room temperature and refrigerate. Garnish with lemon slices.

Cindy Stubblefield
Stafford, Texas

COLD TOMATO SOUP

3 cups tomato juice
2 tablespoons tomato paste
4 scallions, minced
Salt
Pinch of thyme
½ teaspoon curry powder
Grated rind of ½ lemon
2 tablespoons lemon juice
Pepper and sugar to taste
1 cup sour cream
Chopped parsley

Combine all except sour cream and mix well. Chill in refrigerator. Blend in sour cream before serving. Sprinkle each serving with chopped parsley.

Lanelle Jolly
Texas City, Texas

COLD CUCUMBER-YOGURT SOUP

2 large cucumbers, peeled and sliced
½ teaspoon salt
1½ teaspoons sugar
1 tablespoon olive oil
1 cup yogurt
Cucumber slices
Fresh dill

Combine first 5 ingredients in bowl, mixing well. Chill 2 hours or longer. Process in blender 20 seconds. Pour into bowls. Garnish with cucumber slices and fresh dill.

Lanelle Jolly
Texas City, Texas

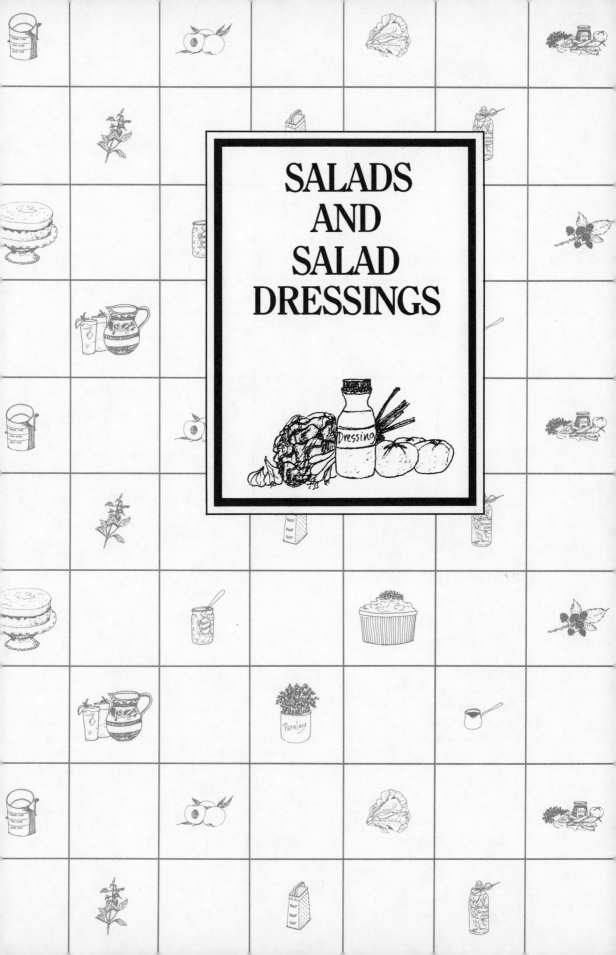

SALADS
AND
SALAD
DRESSINGS

'TATA SALAD

8 *medium-size potatoes*
3 *stalks celery, diced small*
1 *small onion, diced small*
¼ *cup chopped dill pickle*
¼ *cup sweet relish*
1 *cup mayonnaise*
½ *teaspoon dry mustard*
1 *teaspoon salt*
1 *teaspoon black pepper*
3 *hard-boiled eggs, peeled and chopped*

Peel potatoes and dice into ½-inch cubes or smaller. Put in large saucepan, cover with water and bring to a boil. Reduce heat to simmer. Cook just until done—potatoes should still be firm, not mushy. Drain the potatoes. While they cool, mix all the other ingredients together and adjust seasonings to taste. When potatoes are cool, gently mix in with vegetables. Refrigerate overnight or several hours before serving.

Ann Reddehase
Houston, Texas

LAYERED POTATO SALAD

8 *medium Irish potatoes, cooked and peeled*
4 *hard-boiled eggs, sliced*
1 *large onion, chopped fine*

Make a dressing of the following:
8 *ounces sour cream*
1 *to* 1½ *cups mayonnaise*
2 *tablespoons parsley flakes*
1 *teaspoon celery seed*
1 *teaspoon horseradish*
1 *teaspoon salt*

1 *large jar pimientos, chopped fine (save some for garnish)*

In a large salad bowl, arrange a layer of potatoes, then onions, then eggs. Top with some of the dressing. Repeat the layers, adding more dressing. Decorate the top with pimientos.

Mrs. Opal O'Connor
Conroe, Texas

GRANDMA SCHMIDT'S HOT GERMAN POTATO SALAD

8 large potatoes
1 pound bacon, chopped
4 bunches green onions, chopped
3 bell peppers, chopped
1 pint sour cream
Salt and pepper
Garlic powder

Boil potatoes, cool completely, then peel and cut into bite-size pieces. Fry bacon, onions and bell peppers until bacon is brown and onions and peppers are soft. Combine potatoes and bacon mixture in a large pot and add sour cream, seasoning to your own taste. Reheat and serve warm.

Cheryl Ferguson
Hoy, Texas

"This recipe is from my great-grandmother, who grew up in Warda, Texas, in the late 1800's . . . it's a true German potato salad."

HONEYMOON SALAD

Remoulade sauce:
1 teaspoon anchovy paste
½ teaspoon dried tarragon
½ teaspoon lemon pepper
1 teaspoon chopped fresh parsley
1 clove garlic, crushed
1 hard-boiled egg, chopped fine
½ cup mayonnaise

Arrange on two salad plates:
Lettuce
2 tomatoes, quartered
1 avocado, peeled and sliced
¼ cup water chestnuts, sliced
8 black olives, halved
½ pound white crabmeat, flaked

Mix remoulade sauce ingredients and pour over salads.

Judy Fallin
Conroe, Texas

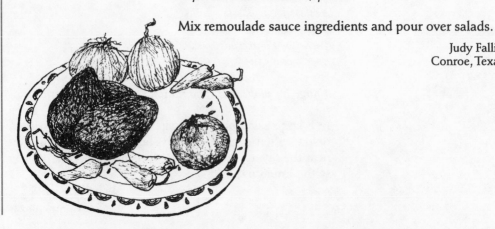

THREE-BEAN SALAD I

1 No. 2 can green beans, drained
1 No. 2 can yellow beans, drained
1 No. 2 can kidney beans, drained
1 medium green pepper, sliced into rings
1 medium onion, sliced into rings
¾ cup sugar
½ cup vinegar
½ cup salad oil
1 teaspoon salt
½ teaspoon pepper

Toss vegetables to mix in a large glass bowl. Make a dressing of sugar, vinegar, oil, salt and pepper; pour over vegetables. Refrigerate overnight. Keep well chilled.

Mrs. J. T. Phillips
Houston, Texas

THREE-BEAN SALAD II

2 15-ounce cans dark red kidney beans
1 15-ounce can green lima beans
2 15-ounce cans cut green beans
¾ cup chopped celery
½ cup chopped bell pepper
½ cup chopped onion
⅓ cup sliced stuffed olives
¼ cup vegetable oil
¼ cup cider vinegar
⅓ cup light molasses
½ teaspoon dry mustard
¼ teaspoon salt
⅛ teaspoon pepper

Drain kidney beans and lima beans, rinse and drain well. Drain green beans. Set all beans aside in colander while other vegetables are being prepared. Stir together the oil, vinegar, molasses, mustard, salt and pepper. Put all beans and vegetables in a container with a tight lid (a half-gallon plastic ice-cream container is ideal). Pour liquid over them, cover and chill several hours or overnight. Occasionally invert container to distribute the liquid to all the contents.

Jeannette Werner
Santa Fe, Texas

MARINATED CUCUMBERS

7 to 9 medium cucumbers, unpeeled and sliced
1 cup onion, sliced and separated
1 cup diced green pepper
1 tablespoon salt
1 teaspoon celery seed
2 cups sugar
1 cup vinegar

Mix all ingredients except sugar and vinegar in one container. Let stand 2 hours. Mix sugar and vinegar in another container and let stand 2 hours. Pour vinegar solution over vegetables and store in refrigator in covered container. Will keep 2–6 months.

Evelyn Remmert
San Antonio, Texas

MARINATED CUCUMBER SALAD

3 cups sliced cucumbers
1 medium green pepper, seeded and cut into rings
1/2 cup green onions, sliced
2 tablespoons vegetable oil
2 tablespoons lemon juice
2 tablespoons vinegar
1 teaspoon sugar
1/4 teaspoon dill weed, crushed

Prepare vegetables. Combine remaining ingredients and pour over vegetables. Toss lightly. Cover and refrigerate 1 hour. Toss lightly several times. Serve in crisp lettuce cups.

Paulette Russek
Lake Jackson, Texas

MOTHER'S SWEET-AND-SOUR SALAD

5 zucchini
1/2 cup celery
1/2 cup green pepper
3 small onions

MARINADE:
3/4 cup sugar
1 teaspoon salt
1/2 cup oil
1/2 teaspoon pepper
1/2 cup vinegar
1/8 cup wine vinegar

Slice vegetables thin. Pour marinade over vegetables and store overnight in the refrigerator, stirring occasionally.

Cynthia Wendel
Danbury, Texas

HOT CHICKEN SALAD

¾ cup cooked and chopped chicken
¾ cup celery, sliced thin
1 tablespoon minced onion
¼ cup walnuts, chopped
⅓ cup mayonnaise
1 tablespoon lemon juice
Salt and pepper
4 slices bread

Combine all ingredients except bread, and mix well. Toast bread on one side. Butter untoasted side and spread with chicken salad. Bake on cookie sheet for 12 minutes at 425°. Serves 4.

Lanelle Jolly
Texas City, Texas

LAYERED HAM SALAD

2 envelopes unflavored gelatin
2 tablespoons sugar
Salt
1 cup water, divided
1¼ cups additional water
4 tablespoons lemon juice, divided
¼ cup vinegar
2 tablespoons chopped green pepper
2 cups finely shredded cabbage
¾ cup mayonnaise
¼ cup minced onion
½ cup chopped sweet pickle
½ cup diced celery
1½ cups finely chopped ham
Salad greens

Combine 1 envelope gelatin, sugar and salt as desired with ½ cup water in saucepan. Heat over low heat until gelatin dissolves, stirring constantly. Remove from heat. Add 1¼ cups water and 2 tablespoons lemon juice along with ¼ cup vinegar. Chill until partly congealed. Fold in pepper and cabbage. Pour into mold. Chill until firm.

Combine 1 envelope gelatin, 2 tablespoons lemon juice, ½ cup water, mayonnaise, and salt to taste. Heat until gelatin dissolves, stirring constantly. Chill until partially congealed. Fold in onion, pickles, celery and ham. Spoon over cabbage layer in mold. Chill until firmly set. Unmold on salad greens. Serves 10.

Lanelle Jolly
Texas City, Texas

TEXAS SHRIMP SALAD

1 pound shrimp, cleaned and cooked
2 hard-boiled eggs, chopped
1 cup chopped celery
½ cup onion
2 tablespoons chopped dill pickles
½ cup mayonnaise
1 tablespoon ketchup
½ teaspoon Worcestershire sauce
Salt and pepper
Lettuce

Combine ingredients and serve on lettuce leaves.

Fern P. Harvey
Palacios, Texas

SPINACH SALAD

2 bags spinach, washed
2 8-ounce cans water chestnuts
4 hard-boiled eggs, chopped
1 can bean sprouts, drained
½ pound bacon, fried crisp and crumbled

DRESSING:
1 cup oil
½ cup sugar
¼ cup vinegar
1 tablespoon Worcestershire sauce
½ cup ketchup
1 medium onion, chopped

Make dressing early in the day or the night before so the flavors blend. Prepare salad ingredients and mix in a large bowl. Pour dressing on spinach salad and toss just before serving.

Rosemary White Kalina
Smithville, Texas

TEXAS GRAPEFRUIT-ORANGE-SPINACH SALAD

1 pound spinach
10 slices bacon
½ pound mushrooms
1 grapefruit, sectioned
1 orange, sectioned

Wash spinach, remove stems, place in towel in refrigerator. Cook and crumble bacon. Clean and slice mushrooms. Peel and section fruit; drain. Add bacon, mushrooms and fruit to spinach and toss with dressing.

DRESSING:
½ cup wine vinegar
2 teaspoons sugar
1 tablespoon grated onion
2 teaspoons Dijon mustard

Whisk together. When smooth, add:
½ cup virgin olive oil
3 tablespoons tahini (ground sesame seeds)

Sprinkle toasted sesame seeds over top after tossing salad.

Janet Kiersted
Houston, Texas

WILD RICE SALAD

⅔ cup uncooked wild rice
2 cups water
½ to 1 teaspoon salt
3 green onions, cut into ½-inch pieces
1 8-ounce can sliced water chestnuts, drained
⅓ cup walnuts, chopped
⅓ cup mayonnaise or salad dressing
Dash of pepper
Lettuce leaves

Wash wild rice in 3 changes of hot water; drain. Combine rice, 2 cups water, and salt in a medium saucepan; bring to a boil. Cover, reduce heat to low, and simmer 30 to 45 minutes or until the rice is tender. Combine cooked rice, onions, water chestnuts, walnuts, mayonnaise and pepper, and stir well. Chill 3 to 4 hours. Serve on lettuce leaves. Serves 8.

Dorothy Burgess
Huntsville, Texas

SAUERKRAUT SALAD

1 can Bavarian-style kraut, drained
½ cup chopped bell pepper
½ cup chopped celery
1 small jar chopped pimientos
2 tablespoons sugar
2 tablespoons vegetable oil
½ teaspoon caraway seed
¼ cup sweet pickle juice

Combine drained sauerkraut with all other ingredients, stirring well. Pack in a glass container and refrigerate overnight. Serves 6.

Helen Anders
La Marque, Texas

BROCCOLI SALAD

1 32-ounce package frozen chopped broccoli
4 hard-boiled eggs, chopped
2 ribs celery, chopped
4 green onions, chopped
½ cup stuffed olives, halved
½ to 1 cup mayonnaise
½ teaspoon lemon pepper
1 tablespoon parsley
1 teaspoon salt

Steam broccoli, cool and chop any large pieces. Add remaining ingredients, mixing well. Chill until ready to serve. Option: Use half broccoli and half cauliflower.

July Fallin
Conroe, Texas

GOOD FOR YOU SALAD

½ cup soaked and drained raisins
3 cups cabbage, finely chopped
2 carrots, grated
1 apple, chopped
½ cup nuts
½ cup mayonnaise
3 tablespoons vinegar
Salt to taste

Soak raisins in hot water in medium-large serving bowl 5 to 6 minutes. Drain. Add remaining ingredients and mix well. Serves 4–6.

Honora L. Arnold
Liberty, Texas

TEXAS CAVIAR

2 14-ounce cans black-eyed peas, drained
1 15-ounce can white hominy, drained
2 medium tomatoes, chopped (optional)
4 green onions, chopped
1 medium-size green pepper, chopped
1 jalapeño pepper, chopped
1 8-ounce bottle commercial Italian dressing

Combine all ingredients except salad dressing. Mix well. Pour salad dressing over black-eyed pea mixture. Cover and marinate at least 2 hours in refrigerator. Drain. Serve as a relish or with tortilla chips.

Joan Lawson
Nacogdoches, Texas

PEA SALAD

2 cans baby English peas, well drained
2 cans white shoe-peg corn

Add:
1 large purple onion, finely chopped
1 medium jar green stuffed olives, sliced
2 medium green bell peppers, chopped
1 stalk celery, peeled and chopped
1 package slivered almonds

Mix with peas and corn, stirring well. Blend together:
½ cup oil
½ cup vinegar
½ cup sugar

Add to above mixture, stir well, and refrigerate. Serve when well marinated.

Loucile Stokes
Humble, Texas

CRANBERRY SALAD

1 package fresh cranberries, grated fine
2 cups sugar
No. 2 can crushed pineapple, drained
¾ package miniature marshmallows
2 cups pecans, chopped fine
1 8-ounce carton Cool Whip

Mix first 5 ingredients together, then add the small carton of Cool Whip. Keeps for weeks in refrigerator.

Mrs. A. B. Cash
Montgomery, Texas

CRANBERRY-JELLO SALAD

1 20-ounce can crushed pineapple
1 6-ounce package cherry Jello
1 cup chopped apple
¾ cup pecans, coarsely broken
1 cup chopped celery
1 14-ounce jar orange-cranberry relish
2 tablespoons lemon juice

Drain pineapple and reserve juice. Add enough water to make 1 cup of juice. Bring juice to boil and add Jello, stirring until dissolved. Set aside to cool, and chop apple, pecans and celery. Add all ingredients to Jello. Pour into an 8½-inch-square pan to congeal. Refrigerate.

Jean Wright
Pasadena, Texas

HEAVENLY HASH

1 8-ounce can crushed pineapple
1 11-ounce can mandarin oranges
1 pound cottage cheese
½ cup chopped pecans
1 12-ounce carton Cool Whip
1 6-ounce package peach-flavored gelatin dessert mix

Drain pineapple and oranges. Mix drained fruit with cottage cheese and pecans. Fold in Cool Whip. Sprinkle with dry gelatin mix on top and refrigerate until time to serve.

Mary Anderson
Richmond, Texas

COOL AND CREAMY FRUIT SALAD

1 8-ounce package cream cheese, softened
2 tablespoons lemon juice
1 teaspoon lemon rind, grated
½ cup whipping cream
¼ cup powdered sugar
2 cups peaches, sliced
2 cups blueberries
2 cups strawberries, sliced
2 cups grapes
2 tablespoons nuts, chopped

Combine cheese, lemon juice and rind, mixing well. Beat whipping cream until soft peaks form. Gradually add sugar and beat until stiff peaks form. Fold into cream-cheese mixture. Layer fruit in bowls. Pour mixture over fruit, then sprinkle with nuts. Chill.

Opal Hayley
La Marque, Texas

MELON FRUIT SALAD

1½ cups yogurt
⅓ cup maple syrup
3 tablespoons toasted sesame seeds
1 teaspoon orange rind
½ teaspoon lemon rind
⅛ teaspoon salt
½ medium-size watermelon
1 cantaloupe
1 honeydew melon
Grapes
Blueberries

Mix yogurt, syrup, sesame seeds, orange rind, lemon rind and salt. Cover and chill. Cut melons with a melon ball cutter, scoop out rest of watermelon to make serving bowl. Cut scallops around the edges of the watermelon rind. Arrange melon balls in shell with grapes and blueberries. Chill until serving time. Spoon yogurt over fruit before serving.

Lanelle Jolly
Texas City, Texas

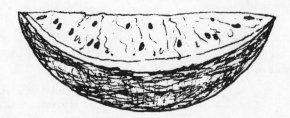

FRUIT-SALAD DRESSING

1 cup sugar
2 tablespoons flour
Pinch salt
1½ cups pineapple juice
Juice of 1 lemon
½ cup orange juice
1 egg, well beaten
½ pint cream, whipped

Mix well the sugar, flour and salt. Add fruit juice and egg. Mix well and cook over medium heat until thick. Chill thoroughly. Fold into whipped cream. Serve over fresh fruit salad.

Lisa McCurry
Huntsville, Texas

CALIFORNIA CREAM

"This is a good substitute for *crème fraîche* that can be made in a moment and is even thicker. Ladle over berries and other fruits, fruit pies, baked apples, etc."

1 egg yolk
4 ounces cream cheese, softened
1 cup sour cream
1 cup whipping cream
2 teaspoons sugar or honey

Place all ingredients in blender or food processor. Whirl just until smooth. Yields 2¼ cups.

Wilma Bruyere
Houston, Texas

CELERY SEED DRESSING

½ cup sugar
1 teaspoon dry mustard
1 teaspoon salt
⅓ cup vinegar
¼ medium onion
1½ teaspoons celery seed
1 cup salad oil

Put first 6 ingredients in blender, and blend well. Slowly add salad oil and blend well. Can be used on a combination salad or slaw.

Ruby Schafer
Houston, Texas

THOUSAND ISLAND DRESSING

1½ cups mayonnaise
½ tablespoon minced onion
1 chopped hard-cooked egg
1 tablespoon chopped pimiento
Dash of cayenne
½ cup thick chili sauce

Mix ingredients thoroughly and chill. Reduced-calorie mayonnaise may be used.

Mrs. H. H. Cherry
Edna, Texas

SPINACH SALAD DRESSING A LA LEE DORMAN

1 cup salad oil
1 cup wine vinegar
¾ cup brown sugar, packed
1 medium onion, grated fine
1 tablespoon Worcestershire sauce
2 teaspoons salt
⅓ to ½ cup ketchup

Mix all ingredients together in a jar and shake each time before using. Toss with well-washed spinach greens. Garnish with crumbled bacon, boiled egg (chopped), fresh mushrooms, etc.

Wilma Bruyere
Houston, Texas

NOTES:

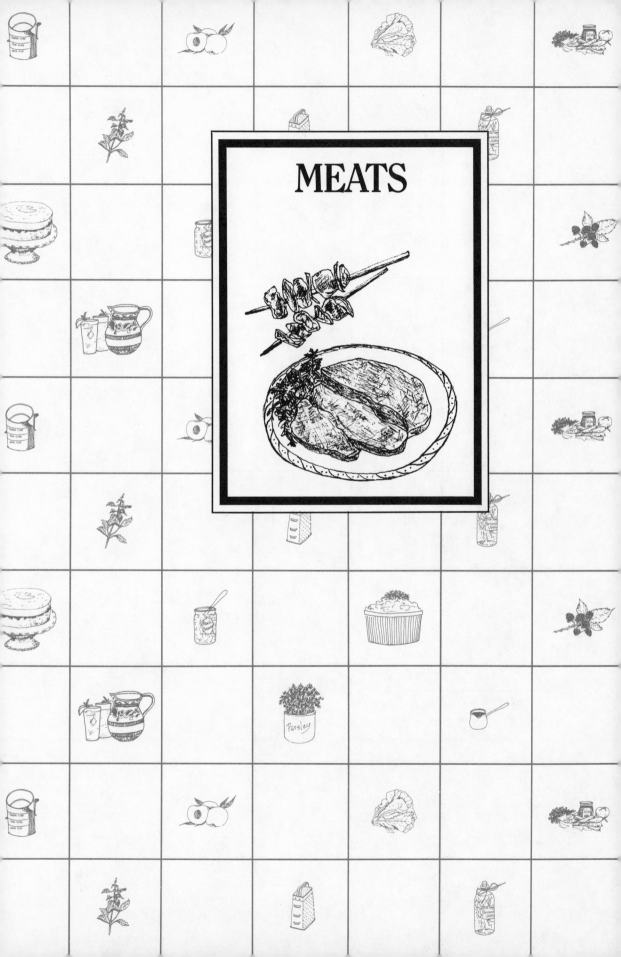

MEATS

CHINESE PEPPER STEAK

1 round steak, tenderized
Salt
Pepper
Garlic seasoning
½ cup margarine or butter
1 teaspoon soy sauce
1 large bell pepper
1 large onion
1 small carton fresh mushrooms
1 small jar pimientos

Cut steak in 2-inch strips; salt and pepper to taste. Sprinkle with garlic seasoning. In large skillet, put enough butter to sear meat. Sear on both sides and add enough water to cook meat until tender. When meat is tender, add remainder of butter, soy sauce, and all vegetables which have been cut in strips lengthwise. Let simmer until vegetables are tender—do not overcook. Serve over rice.

Note: After cooking meat, there should not be any excess water.

Evelyn Shaffer
Baytown, Texas

SWISS STEAK HACIENDA

3 pounds round steak
2 tablespoons flour
2 teaspoons paprika
1 teaspoon garlic salt
½ teaspoon pepper
1 teaspoon chili powder
1 tablespoon wine vinegar
3 tablespoons salad oil, divided
½ cup celery, chopped
½ cup onion, chopped
1 cup red wine
1 cup canned beef broth

Steak should be 1½ to 2 inches thick. Trim excess fat and score on both sides ¼ inch into meat. Combine dry ingredients with wine vinegar and 1 tablespoon oil. Rub into meat. Cover and refrigerate overnight. In large pan brown meat in 2 tablespoons cooking oil on both sides. Add celery, onion, wine and broth. Cover to simmer until fork-tender, about 1¾ hours. Add more broth if necessary. When meat is tender, skim off fat.

Ruth Branch
League City, Texas

BAKED BEEF ROLL

2 cups leftover roast beef or pot roast
1 cup mixed vegetables, cooked
1 small onion
1 cup mushrooms
1 cup rich cream sauce
Salt and pepper
1 batch biscuit dough (see below)
Melted butter
1 egg yolk

Put meat, vegetables, onion and mushrooms through food chopper using medium blade. Make cream sauce by heating 2 tablespoons butter, adding 2 tablespoons flour and 1 cup hot milk, and stirring until smooth. Add this sauce to meat mixture. Stir. Add salt and pepper to taste. Chill while making biscuit dough.

BISCUIT DOUGH:
2 cups flour
3 teaspoons baking powder
½ teaspoon salt
⅓ cup shortening
¾ cup milk

Mix flour, baking powder and salt in a bowl. Cut in shortening; add milk to make a soft dough. Place on floured board and roll out ¼-inch thick. Spread meat mixture on dough and roll up jelly-roll style. Moisten ends to seal. Bake on baking sheet seam side down. Bake at 425° for 25 minutes. Serve with tomato sauce.

Lanelle Jolly
Texas City, Texas

COWBOY SON-OF-A-GUN

"Will feed 10 hungry cowboys. This recipe was used by my ancestors when they came to Texas in the 1820's."

2 pounds stew meat
2 kidneys
½ heart
1 oxtail
1 pound liver
2 pounds beef skirt
1 set sweetbreads
1 pound brains
1 teaspoon salt
½ teaspoon pepper
1 teaspoon chili powder

Cut meat into large chunks (2-inch cubes). In a large stew pot (6-quart), add all ingredients, cover with water and bring to a boil, then simmer for 1½ to 2 hours or until stew thickens. The brains will cook apart and help to thicken the stew. Taste again and you may have to add salt, pepper or chili powder.

Bufford Ashley, Jr.
Sheridan, Texas

HELWEG'S SHINER PICNIC STEW

20 pounds stew meat
2 cups water
2 sticks margarine
15 allspice pods
Salt and pepper

In a very large pot, simmer above ingredients 1 hour. Add:

1 stalk celery, diced
4 onions, chopped
2 cloves garlic, chopped fine
1 bell pepper, chopped
1½ ounces chili powder
1 cup vinegar

Simmer another hour or until meat is tender.

Brian H. Helweg
Shiner, Texas

TEXAS-STYLE ROAST

1 4- to 7-pound brisket or roast, well trimmed
1 tablespoon garlic salt
2 tablespoons celery seed
1 tablespoon pepper
1 tablespoon Accent
1 tablespoon seasoned salt
2 tablespoons Worcestershire sauce
2 tablespoons barbecue sauce (or liquid smoke)

Make a paste of seasonings and sauces. With butter brush, spread paste evenly over all sides and edges of roast. Wrap tightly in foil and let marinate in refrigerator for at least 12 hours. Preheat oven to 300°. Bake in roasting pan without opening foil wrap. Baking time should be: 2 to 3 inches thick, 3 hours; 4 to 5 inches thick, 3½ hours; 6 or more inches , 4 hours.

Neal Nelson
Pasadena, Texas

BACHELOR'S ROAST

1 4-pound beef roast
½ teaspoon pepper
½ teaspoon salt
½ teaspoon minced garlic
3 tablespoons oil
1 small Coke
1 14-ounce bottle ketchup

"A 1950's recipe so easy even a man could cook it right."

Wipe off the roast and score deeply in several places. Mix pepper, salt and minced garlic, and put the mixture in the scored holes. Sear the roast in hot oil. Then drain off oil. Put the roast in a foil-lined roasting pan. Pour 1 small bottle Coke over the meat along with the ketchup. Cover well with foil and put in a 325° oven for 3 hours.

Helen Keggins
Houston, Texas

STEAMED BEEF BRISKET

10 pounds beef brisket
1 teaspoon liquid smoke
3 tablespoons water
1 package dry onion soup mix

Wipe brisket dry and lay in roasting pan. Pour liquid smoke and water in bottom of pan. Spread onion soup mix over top of meat. Cover pan and cook in a 250° oven for 6 hours or in a 225° oven overnight. Refrigerate when done and slice cold. Heat slices in meat juice. Meat juice can also be refrigerated and most of the fat removed when cold.

Sondi Jones
Houston, Texas

FIRESIDE BRISKET

1 whole brisket (about 8 pounds)
2 large cloves garlic, minced
2 large onions, chopped
Pepper
3 tablespoons Worcestershire sauce
2 packages onion soup mix
1 bottle chili sauce
1 can beer
8 carrots, scraped and cut into chunks
3 slices corn rye bread (any bakery)

Rub brisket with garlic and place on bed of chopped onions in a roasting pan with tight-fitting cover or heavy

"This is a great company recipe. Expect raves!"

duty foil. Over the brisket place the following in this order: pepper, Worcestershire sauce, onion soup mix, chili sauce and beer. Lay carrots in pan around brisket. Tear bread into medium pieces and tuck under the brisket, so liquid is covering the bread. Cover and bake in preheated 350° oven for 1 hour. Reduce oven temperature to 275° and braise another 2 to 2½ hours or until done. Remove from oven and let stand until cool. Remove meat and slice. Arrange meat slices and carrots on ovenproof platter; cover with foil.

Make a gravy by taking the bread, half the onions and 2 cups liquid from roasting pan. Place in blender or food processor and process until blended. Return mixture to pan and blend with remaining liquid. About ½ hour before serving, reheat meat and carrots with half the gravy. Pour remainder in gravy boat and pass separately. Serves 12.

Irene Bornet
Houston, Texas

SLOW OVEN STEW

2 pounds stew meat (cut in 1½-inch pieces)
2 medium onions, chopped
3 stalks celery, chopped
4 medium carrots, chopped
1 cup tomato juice
¼ cup quick cooking tapioca
1 tablespoon sugar
Salt and pepper
2 medium potatoes, chopped

Combine all ingredients except potatoes in a 2½-quart casserole. Cover and cook in a slow oven at 300° for 2½ hours. Stir in potatoes and continue cooking covered for 1 more hour or until vegetables are done. Serves 8.

Jean Winters
Burton, Texas

HONEY'S MEAT CASSEROLE

2 onions, chopped
1 clove garlic, minced
2 tablespoons oil
2 pounds ground beef
1 to 2 bell peppers, chopped
1 6-ounce can tomato paste
1½ tablespoons chili powder
1½ tablespoons paprika
Salt and pepper
8 ounces egg noodles, cooked
1 can whole-kernel yellow corn
1 8-ounce can ripe olives, chopped
1 4-ounce can mushrooms
1 cup grated cheddar cheese

"Honey was my grandmother. . . ."

Sauté onion and garlic in oil. Add beef and sauté until brown. Add bell peppers, paste, chili powder, paprika, salt and pepper. Cook 5 minutes, then add noodles, corn, olives and mushrooms. Pour into large casserole dish and top with grated cheese. Bake at 350° for 30 to 45 minutes.

Nita Rivoire
Sugar Land, Texas

LASAGNA

¼ cup olive oil
½ cup chopped onion
1½ teaspoons garlic powder, divided
1 pound lean ground beef
1 6-ounce can tomato paste
2 8-ounce cans peeled tomatoes, sieved
1 cup water
2 8-ounce cans tomato sauce
1 teaspoon oregano
½ teaspoon salt
¼ teaspoon pepper
½ teaspoon sugar
1 pound lasagna noodles
1 pound ricotta cheese
1 egg
1 teaspoon garlic salt
1 tablespoon grated Parmesan cheese
1 pound sliced mozzarella cheese

Heat olive oil in 3-quart saucepan over medium heat. Add onion and ½ teaspoon garlic powder; cook until onions are transparent. Add meat; sauté until lightly browned. Add tomato paste, tomatoes, water and tomato sauce; mix well. Add 1 teaspoon garlic powder, oregano, salt, pepper and sugar. Simmer for 4 hours, stirring occasionally. Boil noodles in rapidly boiling salted water as directed on package. Drain. Mix ricotta cheese, egg, garlic salt and Parmesan cheese.

Line bottom of greased 8-inch baking dish with ½ cup meat sauce. Top with layer of noodles, mozzarella cheese and ricotta cheese mixture. Repeat again, starting with sauce and ending with the ricotta mixture, making three layers. Top with sauce and mozzarella cheese. Bake in preheated 350° oven for 25 minutes, or until bubbling. Let stand for 5 to 10 minutes before cutting. Serves 6 to 8.

Margaret Nelson
Baytown, Texas

CHEESE-BURGERS

Allow ¼ pound ground beef for each hamburger, pressing it into 2 thin patties. For filling, cream together the following:

¼ pound butter
¼ pound Roquefort cheese (or any sharp cheese)
3 tablespoons prepared mustard

The filling is enough for 8 hamburgers. Spread on one patty, leaving ½ inch around edge for sealing. Top with second patty, pressing edges together. Broil on each side. Serve on toasted hamburger buns.

Gladys Pennison
Houston, Texas

TEXAS HASH

2 large onions, sliced
2 green peppers, sliced thin
3 tablespoons shortening
1 pound ground beef
2 cups canned tomatoes
½ cup uncooked rice
1 teaspoon chili powder
¼ teaspoon pepper

Cook onions and green peppers slowly in shortening until onions are yellow. Add beef and sauté until the mixture falls apart. Add tomatoes, rice and seasonings. Arrange in large casserole, cover and bake in moderately hot oven (375°). Bake for 45 minutes or until done. Serves 8.

Dorothy Lee
La Marque, Texas

SCHWEINE-FLEISCH-PASTETE MEAT PIE

4 or 5 pounds pork loin strip
2 or 3 cloves garlic, chopped fine
Salt
Pepper
Chili pequins (small red peppers)
Vinegar

Cut pork into small cubes and layer meat, garlic, salt, pepper, red peppers and vinegar in a stone crock. Make sure mixture is covered with vinegar and pressed down with a saucer. Refrigerate for at least 2 weeks. Stir occasionally and add vinegar if necessary.

This mixture is baked in a double crust pie. The top crust should be brushed with a beaten egg and baked in a 300° oven until lightly brown. The meat mixture will keep in the refrigerator for several months and the above amount will make about 6 pies. The pie should be cut in small wedges and is delicious served either hot or cold. This is a third generation recipe.

"This recipe has been prepared by my mother, Mrs. Kemper Williams, Sr. . . . She is in her early 80's and continues to make these 'pies' annually."

Kemper Williams, Jr.
Victoria, Texas

HOPPIN' JOHN

1 cup chopped ham
1 cup onion, finely chopped
½ teaspoon hot pepper sauce
2 tablespoons oil
2 cans black-eyed peas, heated
½ teaspoon salt
3 cups rice, cooked
Ham slices
Mustard greens

Sauté chopped ham, onions and hot pepper sauce in oil over moderate heat for 3 to 5 minutes, stirring frequently, until the onions are soft, but not yet brown. Combine black-eyed peas, ham mixture, salt and cooked rice. Heat thoroughly. Garnish with thin slices of ham and mustard greens. Serves 8.

Eloise Moore
Houston, Texas

HAM PIE

2 or 3 potatoes, chopped
1 large onion, chopped
1 stalk celery, chopped
1 small green pepper, chopped
3 cups of chopped ham
6 boiled eggs, chopped
1 can cream of celery soup
Biscuit dough

Boil potatoes with onions and other vegetables; drain, reserving liquid. Put vegetables, ham and eggs in baking dish and add 1 can of cream of celery soup. Add enough cooking liquid from vegetables to keep ingredients moist. Top with biscuit crust and bake until brown.

Lenore Gammage
Brenham, Texas

BAKED PORK CHOPS

8 boneless pork chops
2 tablespoons prepared mustard
Salt and pepper
Italian-style bread crumbs
1 stick butter or margarine
1 can cream of mushroom soup
1 can cream of chicken soup
1 cup water

Rub both sides of chops with mustard, salt and pepper. Roll chops in bread crumbs. Melt butter in skillet. Brown chops in butter and place in baking dish. Combine soups, and water in a bowl. Pour over chops. Bake at 300° for 1 hour and 30 minutes. Serves 8.

Margaret Nelson
Baytown, Texas

BARBECUED SPARERIBS

3 to 4 pounds ribs
1 lemon
1 large onion
1 cup ketchup
1/3 cup Worcestershire sauce
1 teaspoon chili powder
1 teaspoon salt
2 dashes Tabasco sauce
2 cups water

Place ribs in pan, meaty side up. On each piece, place a slice of unpeeled lemon and a slice of onion. Roast in

450° oven for 30 minutes. Combine remaining ingredients and bring to a boil. Pour over ribs and continue baking at 350° until tender—about 45 to 60 minutes. Baste ribs every 15 minutes. If sauce gets too thick, add more water.

Irene Madvig
Spring, Texas

WADE'S POLISH SAUSAGE AND POTATOES

1 ring of Polish sausage
7 medium potatoes, peeled
1 medium onion
2 cans tomato sauce
Salt and pepper

Cut sausage into small pieces. Place in deep skillet and cook for 5 minutes. Cut potatoes into small strips and chop onion into small pieces. Add to cooked sausage. Let mixture cook until potatoes soften, then add tomato sauce and let simmer 15 minutes. Season to taste with salt and pepper.

J. T. Wade
Gilmer, Texas

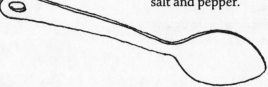

VENISON BACKSTRAP AU POIVRE

1 pound venison backstrap (tenderloin of deer)
Coarsely ground black pepper
4 tablespoons soy sauce
2 or 3 tablespoons margarine
1 cup beef broth
½ cup red wine
Chopped fresh parsley

Cut venison into 1-inch steaks. Press pepper into both sides of steaks. Marinate in soy sauce at least 2 hours at room temperature. Turn occasionally. Melt margarine in skillet. Sauté steak 2 to 3 minutes on each side, turning once. Remove to serving platter and keep warm (do not let steaks cook anymore—they must be rare or they may be tough). Stir soy sauce from marinade, beef broth and wine into pan drippings remaining in skillet and reduce to 1 cup. Pour over steaks. Sprinkle with fresh parsley.

Barbara N. Larrabee
Houston, Texas

TEXAS VENISON STEAKS

2−4 venison steaks
Seasoned meat tenderizer
½ cup Wishbone Italian salad dressing
Salt and pepper
Flour for dredging
Oil for frying

Sprinkle steaks with seasoned tenderizer. Pour salad dressing over steaks and marinate overnight. Do not wash sauce off steaks. Salt and pepper the steaks as desired. Flour both sides of steaks. Heat frying pan with oil until hot. Put steaks in oil and brown on both sides. Line a 9×13×2-inch pan with aluminum foil. As each steak is browned on both sides in the frying pan, remove and place in the lined pan, and cover with foil. Place pan in oven heated to 250° for 1 hour. If steaks seem too dry, add a small amount of water and reduce heat to 200°. Steaks produce their own gravy if not cooked too fast.

For barbecued venison, grill marinated steaks over hot coals.

Lottie Lehmann
Dickinson, Texas

SWEET-AND-SOUR LAMB CHOPS

6 lamb chops
¼ cup peanut oil
¼ cup vinegar
¼ cup brown sugar
1 teaspoon salt
⅛ teaspoon pepper
¼ teaspoon ginger
1 medium orange, sliced
1 medium lemon, cut in wedges

Brown lamb chops slowly on each side in peanut oil. Combine vinegar, brown sugar, salt, pepper and ginger. Mix well and pour over chops. Arrange orange and lemon over chops. Cover and cook over low heat for about 30 minutes, or until chops are tender. Serves 4−6.

Marilyn Egleston
Needville, Texas

A MAN'S BARBECUE SAUCE

2¼ cups ketchup
2¼ cups water
2 teaspoons instant beef broth
1¼ teaspoons dry mustard
1 tablespoon chili powder
1 teaspoon black pepper
¼ teaspoon cayenne pepper
½ teaspoon garlic powder
½ teaspoon salt
2 teaspoons Worcestershire sauce
2 shakes liquid red-pepper sauce
3 tablespoons brown sugar
½ teaspoon liquid smoke
1 tablespoon lemon juice

Bring everything to boil, reduce heat and simmer, stirring occasionally, 15 minutes. Cool to room temperature. Makes 1 quart.

Chester N. Peden
Arcadia, Texas

BARBECUE SAUCE I

2 medium onions
4 tablespoons butter
4 tablespoons brown sugar
2 cups ketchup
2 tablespoons dry mustard
1 cup water
1 teaspoon garlic powder
1 teaspoon pepper
1 tablespoon Tabasco
1 can chicken broth (for chicken or game birds) or
    1 can beef bouillon (for beef, pork, or venison)
8 tablespoons lemon juice
½ cup fresh chopped parsley
2 tablespoons Worcestershire sauce
2 teaspoons salt

Grind onions in food chopper, and brown well in butter. Add remaining ingredients and simmer for 30 minutes.

Joe Blake & His Pals
Liberty, Texas

BARBECUE SAUCE II

Juice of 2 large lemons
1 cup cooking oil
2 cups vinegar
2 teaspoons red pepper
2 tablespoons dry mustard
2 cups water
2 tablespoons Worcestershire sauce
1 teaspoon garlic powder
Black pepper, salt and seasoning salt to taste

Boil the above ingredients for 30 minutes, adding the lemons you squeezed the lemon juice from.

R. W. Smith
Houston, Texas

SOUTHERN BARBECUE SAUCE

½ cup butter
1 sour pickle, chopped
2 tablespoons onion, chopped
2 tablespoons Worcestershire sauce
2 tablespoons chili sauce
4 slices lemon
1 tablespoon brown sugar
1 green pepper, chopped
1 cup vinegar

Combine all ingredients and mix thoroughly. Simmer in saucepan until butter melts, stirring occasionally. Makes 1¾ cups, or enough for 2 or 3 chickens. Also good on pork and lamb.

Sondi Jones
Houston, Texas

MOPPING SAUCE

1 pint good cooking oil
½ ounce garlic juice
½ ounce onion juice
2 ounces lemon juice

Combine all ingredients. When meat starts to look dry, spray-on sauce with bottle-type sprayer, or brush with small cloth mop.

Joe Blake & His Pals
Liberty, Texas

MOP SAUCE

For brisket, chicken, ham or anything slow-smoked on an outdoor grill.

1 quart water
2 cups white vinegar
½ cup butter
1 lemon, sliced thin
1 onion, sliced thin
2 tablespoons black pepper
2 tablespoons salt
1 can or bottle beer (optional)

Mix all ingredients in a large pot (one that can be put on outdoor grill) and cook over high heat until mixture starts to boil and onion gets soft. Then put on grill to keep warm and use frequently and generously to baste meats that are smoking. It tenderizes, flavors, and keeps meat moist as it cooks.

Doug Reddehase
Houston, Texas

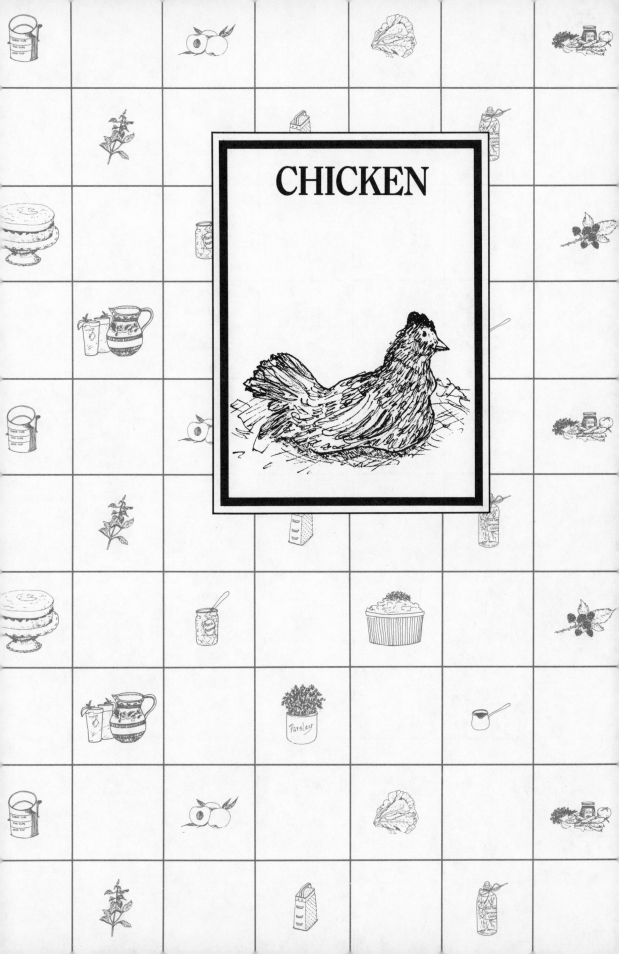

CHICKEN

FRENCH CHICKEN

1 frying chicken, cut in pieces
1 8-ounce carton sour cream
1 cup white wine
1 teaspoon thyme

Season chicken with salt and pepper. Sauté chicken until light brown. Arrange pieces in baking dish. Mix sour cream and wine. Pour over chicken. Sprinkle with thyme and bake for 1 hour at 350°.

Jimmie Gray Durdin
Houston, Texas

HONEY FRENCH CHICKEN

1 large frying chicken, cut up
¼ cup oil
¼ cup apple cider vinegar
¼ cup bottled chili sauce
¼ cup honey
1 teaspoon Worcestershire sauce

Put all ingredients, except chicken, in jar and shake well. Place chicken in baking dish and bake at 350° for 30 minutes with ⅓ mixture. After 30 minutes turn chicken and add more of the mixture. Bake another 30 minutes, basting occasionally with remaining sauce.

L. James
Houston, Texas

EASY CHICKEN CORDON BLEU

8 boneless chicken fillets (about 2 pounds)
8 teaspoons chopped fresh parsley
8 slices (4 ounces) mozzarella cheese
4 slices (4 ounces) thin-sliced boiled ham, cut in half
1 tablespoon mayonnaise
1 tablespoon warm water
¼ cup seasoned bread crumbs

Pound fillets until thin. Lay out flat and sprinkle with parsley. Top with cheese slice, then ham slice and roll up. Secure with toothpick if necessary. Stir together mayonnaise and water. Roll each fillet in mayonnaise mixture, then in bread crumbs. Arrange fillets, seam side down, on a greased baking sheet. Bake at 425° for 15 to 20 minutes.

Lisa McCurry
Huntsville, Texas

UPPER-CRUST CHICKEN

10 slices day-old white bread
2 cups chicken, cooked and chopped
1 cup chopped celery
2 cups shredded cheddar cheese
1 cup mayonnaise
2 eggs, slightly beaten
1/2 teaspoon poultry seasoning
1/2 teaspoon lemon pepper
1/2 teaspoon salt
1 1/2 cups milk

Trim crusts from bread and reserve. Cut bread slices diagonally into quarters. Cut reserved crusts into cubes. Combine cubes, chicken, celery and 1¾ cups cheese; mix well. Spoon into 12×8-inch buttered baking dish. Arrange bread quarters over chicken mixture. Combine mayonnaise, eggs and seasonings and mix well. Gradually add milk, mixing until well blended. Pour over bread and sprinkle with remaining cheese. Cover and refrigerate overnight. Bake uncovered at 375° for 35 to 40 minutes. Serves 4.

Judy Fallin
Conroe, Texas

CHICKEN NOODLE CASSEROLE

1 3-pound fryer chicken, cooked, deboned and chopped
1 medium onion, chopped
3 or 4 stalks celery, chopped
1/4 cup oil
2 cans cream of mushroom soup
2 cans cream of chicken soup
1 can evaporated milk
1 large can chow mein noodles (5 ounces)
1 stick margarine, melted
2 1/2 cups Pepperidge Farm stuffing mix

Sauté onions and celery in oil until tender. Combine chicken, onions, celery, soups, canned milk and noodles in a large casserole dish. Mix melted margarine and stuffing mix. Sprinkle over casserole. Bake at 350° for 40 minutes.

Irene Farr
Pasadena, Texas

CHICKEN PIE

½ cup diced onion
½ cup diced celery
5 tablespoons butter
4 tablespoons flour
2 cups chicken broth
2 to 3 cups stewed chicken, diced
1 10-ounce package frozen peas
¾ cup diced and cooked carrots
½ cup chopped mushrooms (optional)
¾ cup additional broth
½ teaspoon sage
1 tablespoon granulated bouillon
Pie crust

Sauté onion and celery in butter. Add flour, stirring until well blended. Slowly add 2 cups broth, cooking until thickened and smooth. Season with salt and pepper, then set aside. In a flat baking dish, layer diced chicken, peas, carrots and mushrooms. Pour the broth mixture over the top, then add ¾ cup broth, sage and bouillon granules. Top with pie crust and slash the top. Bake at 425° until done and brown on top.

Hildreth Angus
Seminole, Texas

GREEN CHILI CHICKEN

1 large fryer
1 medium onion, chopped
1 can cream of mushroom soup
½ pint sour cream
1 can green chilies, chopped
½ cup milk
½ cup chicken broth
½ pound cheddar cheese, grated
1 bag tortilla chips

Boil and debone chicken, then cut into bite-size pieces. In a bowl combine onion, soup, sour cream, chilies, milk and chicken broth. Put a layer of tortilla chips on bottom of casserole. Add a layer of chicken mixture, then cheese; repeat layers. Bake 30 minutes at 350°.

Monica McClung
Garland, Texas

CHICKEN AND PEPPERS

1 onion, chopped small
1 cup chopped bell pepper
3 chicken breasts, cooked and cut into pieces
1½ cans cream of mushroom soup
2 cans green chilies, chopped
2 cups shredded cheddar cheese
2 cups sour cream
1¾-pound bag tortilla chips, crushed

Sauté onion and green pepper in a little oil until tender. After cooling slightly, mix with all other ingredients except chips. In 9×13-inch pan spread ½ bag crushed chips on bottom. Place chicken mixture on top, then add the rest of the crushed chips on top of mixture. Bake at 350° for 40 minutes or until hot.

Terry Davis
Austin, Texas

CHICKEN DELIGHT

3 cups cooked chicken
1 cup mayonnaise
1½ cups chopped celery
3 tablespoons chopped bell pepper
1 cup grated cheddar cheese
¼ cup chopped onion
½ cup slivered almonds
Salt and pepper

Mix all ingredients except ¼ cup almonds. Place in a casserole dish and top with almonds. Bake at 350° for 25 minutes. Add remaining almonds; bake an additional 5 minutes. Serves 4 to 6.

Donna R. Grabs
Austin, Texas

CHICKEN-CORNBREAD CASSEROLE

4 cups crumbled cornbread
½ cup chopped green or white onion
½ cup chopped celery
2 cups chicken, cooked and coarsely chopped
2 cups chicken broth
1 can cream of chicken soup, undiluted

Mix all ingredients together, pour into a 12×8×2-inch baking dish. Bake at 350° for 45 minutes. Serves 8.

Josephine Miller Bush
Huntsville, Texas

CHICKETTI

1 4- to 5-pound stewing chicken
1 teaspoon salt
6 cups water
2 onions, chopped
1 28-ounce can tomatoes
½ teaspoon black pepper
Salt
¾ cup chopped celery
1 teaspoon garlic powder
½ teaspoon paprika
2 bay leaves
2 cans chicken broth
1 9-ounce package spaghetti
2 cans cream of chicken soup
2 cups grated cheese

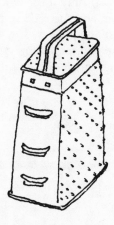

Cook chicken in salted water until tender. Remove from liquid and debone. Cut into small pieces. Put onions, tomatoes, pepper, salt, celery, garlic powder, bay leaves and paprika in pot with liquid. Add one can of chicken broth. Cook until the vegetables are tender. Return chicken to pot. Add can of broth and spaghetti. Simmer until tender. Add cream of chicken soup and grated cheese. Mix lightly and serve. Serves 12.

Lanelle Jolly
Texas City, Texas

ARROZ CON POLLO, PUERTO RICO STYLE

1 medium onion
1 large bell pepper
1 clove garlic
1 pinch cumin
1 can whole tomatoes
10 green olives
15 capers
2 tablespoons oil
1 whole chicken, cut up
4½ cups rice

Blend first 7 ingredients in a blender. Heat oil in a pan. Pour in mixture, bring to a boil, add cut-up chicken and let it simmer until almost cooked. Add rice; lower flame. Cook 10 more minutes or until rice is done.

Crispina Babbitt
Austin, Texas

ROBIN HOOD'S CHICKEN

3 tablespoons cooking oil
2- to 3-pound fryer, cut up
1 clove garlic, minced
2 teaspoons salt
½ teaspoon black pepper
1 cup water
1 cup chopped onion
2 cups cooked peas and carrots (fresh, frozen or canned)
3 cups rice, cooked
2 tablespoons ketchup (optional)

Heat cooking oil in large skillet. Add chicken pieces and brown on all sides. Add the garlic, 1 teaspoon of the salt and ¼ teaspoon of the black pepper. Turn the heat down and cook slowly about 30 minutes or until the chicken is tender. Add a small amount of water only if the chicken cooks dry. When chicken is tender, add the onions, peas and carrots, and the remaining salt and pepper. Top with the cooked rice. Combine ketchup and remaining water; pour over rice. Cover and cook until most of the liquid is absorbed. Serves 6.

Allene Eberle
Porter, Texas

Parsley

SKILLET CHICKEN IN ASPARAGUS SAUCE

¼ cup butter
1 egg
1½ pounds boneless chicken breast fillets
½ cup flour
1 teaspoon white pepper
1 can cream of asparagus soup
1 cup milk
2 carrots, peeled, cut in 2-inch sections, then quartered
Fresh asparagus

Melt butter in large skillet. Beat egg in a medium size bowl. Place chicken in egg and prick breast with fork. Mix flour and pepper in shallow dish; coat both sides of chicken breast. Place chicken in skillet on low temperature; brown both sides, turning frequently for 15 minutes. In a small bowl combine soup and milk; whisk until smooth. Add soup mixture and carrots to skillet. Cook covered on low temperature for 45 minutes. Turn chicken often. Garnish with fresh steamed asparagus spears in season. Serves 4.

Jo Adele Hughes
Houston, Texas

GOLDEN CHICKEN AND RICE

1 medium onion
2 stalks celery
2 tablespoons flour
¼ stick margarine
1 chicken, boiled and deboned (save broth)
1 can golden mushroom soup
1 small jar pimientos
Salt and pepper

Sauté onion, celery and flour in the margarine. Boil and debone chicken and place in the chicken broth. Add sautéed mixture to broth, then add the golden mushroom soup, pimientos, salt and pepper. Simmer for 30 minutes. Serve with rice.

Carolyn Chafin
Sweeny, Texas

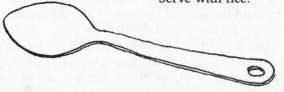

CHICKEN KABOBS

2 packages frozen skinless chicken, cut into ½- to 1-inch cubes
½ cup soy sauce
¼ cup melted butter
2 limes, juice only
2 tablespoons Tabasco sauce
¾ cup Worcestershire sauce
1 can beer (dark is best)
Pepper
Salt
⅛ teaspoon paprika
¼ cup onion flakes
¼ cup garlic powder
2 bell peppers, sliced in 2-inch squares
3 small white onions, quartered
1 package large mushrooms, cut in half
4 small tomatoes, quartered.

Cut chicken while still partially frozen for ease in cutting. Mix next 11 ingredients and pour over chicken; marinate 2 to 8 hours in refrigerator.

Wash and prepare vegetables. Place chicken and vegetables on metal skewers and cook over charcoal grill for about 20 minutes. Rotate every 5 minutes and baste with marinade each time. Serve over rice or with salad.

B. J. Joyce
San Marcos, Texas

CHICKEN AND DUMPLINGS I

EDITOR'S NOTE:
The response to Ron Stone's request for chicken and dumplings recipes was overwhelming. These are only a few of the many we received.

1 large fryer (3½ to 4 pounds)
8 cups hot water
Salt and pepper
2 cups flour
1 teaspoon salt
⅛ teaspoon soda
2 tablespoons shortening, melted
1 egg
⅔ cup buttermilk
1 stick butter
Black pepper

Place chicken in hot water. Let it come to a boil. Turn to low heat and cook until done, about 1 hour. Turn off the heat and leave the chicken in broth for about 30 minutes.

Sift flour, salt and soda together. Put shortening and egg in center of flour. Add small amount of buttermilk as needed, using a fork to mix with until all of flour has blended to make dough. Flour a pastry cloth or wax paper and knead dough using plenty of flour. Roll very thin and cut in short strips.

Remove chicken from broth and place in casserole dish. Bring broth to rolling boil and drop strips one piece at a time until all have been dropped into the broth. Turn heat to low and add butter and black pepper. Put lid on pot and let simmer about 15 minutes. When done, pour hot dumplings over the chicken.

Elna Cummins
Cleveland, Texas

CHICKEN AND DUMPLINGS II

1 chicken
1 small onion
2 cups flour
¼ cup shortening
1 egg
½ teaspoon soda
½ teaspoon salt
¾ to 1 cup buttermilk

Boil chicken and onion until chicken is tender. Bone chicken and cut into bite-size pieces. Mix flour, shortening, egg, soda, salt and buttermilk to make dumpling batter. Roll dough thin and cut into strips. Drop into boiling broth and cover and cook until tender. Keep cover on while cooking. Return chicken to hot pot, or pour hot dumplings and broth over warm chicken.

Lou Wilson
Alvin, Texas

DUMPLINGS TO FREEZE

"If you like chewy type dumplings, please try this recipe."

1 stick margarine
1 teaspoon salt
2 cups boiling water
4 cups flour

Put margarine in boiling salted water, and bring just to boiling. Put flour in mixing bowl. Pour hot mixture over flour and mix well. Knead to a nice dough. Place on a well-floured surface, rolling as thin as you like, and cut into squares or strips as desired. Place on a cookie sheet in freezer until frozen, so they won't stick together. Then place in a container and return to freezer. Use as desired.

Mrs. George Murphy

TEJAS DUMPLINGS

1¾ cups flour, sifted
¼ cup maíz, sifted (Mexican-style cornmeal)
1 large pinch garlic salt
1 tablespoon crushed red chili pepper
1 tablespoon pepper
4 medium green onions, sautéed
2 cups grated queso de chivo (goat cheese) or mild white
      cheese

Simmer the broth that a whole chicken has been boiled in. Combine both flours, garlic salt, crushed red chili and black pepper in a separate bowl until blended. Add 1 spoonful at a time of simmering broth until desired consistency, sticky but well bonded. Place into broth 1 tablespoon of dumpling mix at a time, simmering until all are done. Garnish chicken and dumplings with onion and cheese.

Hugh Bob Majors
Huntsville, Texas

L-C CAFETERIA'S CHICKEN AND DUMPLINGS

1 3- to 4-pound chicken hen
1 bay leaf
½ cup chicken fat, butter, or margarine
1 cup chopped onion
¾ cup chopped celery
¼ cup chopped bell pepper
¼ cup chopped parsley
Salt and pepper
Monosodium glutamate (MSG)
Yellow food coloring

DUMPLINGS:
3 cups flour
1 teaspoon baking powder
1 teaspoon salt
4 tablespoons shortening
3 eggs
½ cup cold water
½ cup additional flour

Parsley

". . . this recipe came from the old L-C Cafeteria, on Main Street [in Houston], and was considered the best around. I don't know about that, but I know that I sure had a lot of drop-in company when I made a potful, and never had to worry about leftovers. I still use this recipe, but wouldn't dream of using ½ cup of fat to sauté the vegetables in. We've found that we can get by with a lot less fat these days without sacrificing flavor, but then this isn't a low-calorie dish, at best. I have also found that the addition of a little rubbed sage and poultry seasoning makes the flavor even better."

Cook hen in water to cover with bay leaf and any other preferred seasonings until tender. Remove meat from bones, and dice to obtain at least 4 cups of meat; refrigerate.

Concentrate or extend broth to obtain 3 quarts. Sauté in chicken fat the onion, celery, bell pepper and parsley; add to broth and simmer until tender. Add salt, pepper, MSG and food coloring to broth and let simmer until ready for dumplings.

To make dumplings, sift together into a bowl the 3 cups of flour, baking powder and salt. Cut in the shortening. Blend in the eggs and ½ cup cold water, mixing to produce a soft, sticky dough. Turn dough out on board and work in ½ cup additional flour; work quickly to make a soft, rollable dough.

Roll dough to a ⅛-inch thickness. Cut into 1-inch strips, then into 2-inch lengths. Drop dumplings 1 at a time into boiling broth. When all are added, broth may be thickened if needed by stirring in a paste made of ⅓ cup flour and ½ cup water.

Cover and simmer dumplings ½ to 1 hour. Add cold diced chicken just in time to heat before serving.

Jan J. Phillips
League City, Texas

PAPA'S SPECIAL DUMPLINGS

3 cups flour
1½ teaspoons salt
1½ teaspoons baking powder
½ teaspoon soda
1 cup buttermilk
1 cup milk
Black pepper

Flour hands and mix first 5 ingredients. Roll out ¼-inch thick. Drop the well-floured dumplings into hot chicken broth to which 1 cup of milk has been added. Cook 10 minutes or so. Use plenty of pepper.

Mary Anderson
Richmond, Texas

MYRTLE'S CHICKEN AND DUMPLINGS

"This one is unique, in that it is so simple and receives high compliments when served."

2½ cups flour
1 cup cold water
½ teaspoon salt

Boil your choice of chicken pieces in plenty of water seasoned to taste. Make a stiff dough of the flour, water and salt. Let sit 4 to 6 hours.(The secret is having the dough sit a long time.) Roll out thin and cut into small pieces; slowly drop 1 at a time into the boiling broth, stretching each piece paper-thin. Boil about 15 minutes.
   Note: Chicken may be boned before dropping in dumplings, but it is not essential.

Myrtle Robertson
Houston, Texas

CZECH DUMPLINGS I

1 cup flour
1 teaspoon butter
1 egg
Milk

Mix flour, butter and egg. Add enough milk to make a dough about as thick or just a bit thicker than biscuit dough. Dough should be beaten until very smooth. Roll out on a floured board to ¼-inch thickness. Cut into desired pieces and drop into chicken broth that is gently boiling. (I remove the meat before I put the dumplings in.) Boil about 15 minutes, stirring with a wooden spoon occasionally.

Mrs. W. C. Regmund
Bryan, Texas

CZECH DUMPLINGS II

2 cups flour
2 level teaspoons baking powder
2 eggs
1 tablespoon butter, melted
1 slice bread, crumbled into melted butter

Sift together the flour and baking powder. Break the eggs into the flour mixture. Then add enough milk to make a dough that handles easily. Beat well. Place dough on a floured board and knead in buttered crumbs. Knead with hand until smooth. Cut dough in 2 pieces or more if desired. Shape into round loaves, pinching the dough together well so that the dumpling will not lose its shape while cooking. Boil in an uncovered pot of water which is gently boiling for 15 or 20 minutes, stirring occasionally with a wooden spoon. Slice into desired number of slices as soon as taken out of water. These are good with sauerkraut or chicken gravy. If left over, put in a steamer and heat.

Mrs. W. C. Regmund
Bryan, Texas

COUNTRY CHICKEN AND DUMPLINGS

1 3- to 4-pound chicken
Water
Salt and pepper
2 eggs
⅔ cup milk
3 tablespoons fat from broth
1 teaspoon baking powder
1 teaspoon salt
Flour

"Chicken and dumplings was usually the highlight of Sunday dinner after coming home from church."

Cook chicken with enough water to cover, adding salt and pepper as desired. Cook slowly until chicken is tender. Remove chicken from broth. Beat eggs, and add milk, chicken fat, baking powder, salt and enough flour to make a stiff dough. Roll out to ⅛-inch thickness. Cut into squares and allow to dry. Drop into boiling broth, and cook slowly for 20 to 30 minutes. Stir occasionally.

Audrey T. McShan
Tomball, Texas

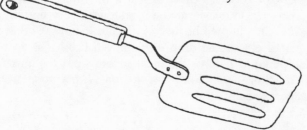

SOUTHERN DUMPLINGS

2 cups sifted flour
1 teaspoon salt
1 teaspoon baking powder
1 tablespoon shortening
Chicken broth

"This is copied exactly as it appears in an old cookbook. I skip the flour sifting and use fryer parts or boney pieces of chicken. The broth has to be cooled to add to the dry ingredients. For better flavor, I add 1 or 2 bouillon cubes to broth before dropping dumplings in; add black pepper to taste."

Sift the flour, salt and baking powder together. Cut in the shortening and gradually add about ⅔ cup of chicken broth, until a stiff dough results. Roll out on a floured board and cut into 1-inch-wide strips. Drop a few at a time into the remaining chicken broth, which has been brought to a boil. Cover and cook for 10 to 15 minutes. Serves 6.

Mamie Anthony
Nacogdoches, Texas

CHICKEN 'N DUMPLIN'S

"This is our family favorite. My husband's mama taught me to make them like she was taught back in Mississippi."

Place *onion* in cavity of large *chicken,* cover with *water,* and boil until tender. Remove chicken from broth and set aside to cool. When cool, remove bones and skin from meat and separate into small pieces.

Prepare dumplin' dough: Sift together *3 cups flour, 3 teaspoons baking powder* and *1 teaspoon salt.* Cut in *6 tablespoons shortening.* Mix *1 egg* with *1 cup milk* and stir into flour mixture, making a soft dough. Divide dough into 3 parts, lightly knead, and let set for a few minutes.

Add water to broth to make about 5 to 6 quarts. Bring to a boil. Roll out first ball of dough a little thicker than pie crust. Cut into 1-inch strips. When broth comes to a rolling boil, pinch strips into about 2-inch pieces and drop into broth. They will come to the top and float. When top of broth is covered with pieces, cover and let cook for a few minutes. (Be sure to use a deep pot or they'll run over.) Add another layer of strips, allowing each layer to cook a little. If you must stir, do so gently or dumplin's will break apart.

When all strips are done, add chicken. Turn heat down very low, cover the pot, and simmer until dumplin's are done all through. If you need to add liquid, heat a little milk with a little butter and stir into pot. Salt and pepper to taste.

Pat M. Woods
West Columbia, Texas

CORNBREAD DRESSING

Cornbread (2 large iron skilletfuls)
2 medium onions, diced
1 complete bunch of celery, diced (with leaves)
1 small bell pepper, diced
4 tablespoons oil
6 or 7 slices stale white bread
2 cups chicken broth
6 eggs
1 tablespoon poultry seasoning
1 teaspoon dried sage or sage leaves
Salt and pepper
¼ cup chopped parsley

Cook cornbread and allow to cool. Crumble it into a large bowl. After all the onions, celery and pepper are diced, sauté in the oil until the onions are translucent. Add vegetables to the cornbread. Cube the white bread and add to mixture. Add the chicken broth and mix well. If you are baking a chicken or turkey, add any drippings that cook off of them to dressing mixture. The juicier the uncooked dressing the better the cooked dressing. After adding the broth and juice, mix in 6 eggs very well. Add all the seasonings and parsley. Keep stirring until everything is very well mixed. More sage can be added to your taste, or some left out if you don't care for it. Pour dressing into a roasting pan and bake about 1 hour or until dressing is set.

Sandra Hollis
Huntsville, Texas

OLD-FASHIONED CORNBREAD STUFFING

1 cup boiling stock
2 cups cornbread crumbs
1 cup finely chopped celery
1 cup finely chopped onion
Salt
Pepper
Sage to taste
3 eggs, raw
2 hard-boiled eggs, coarsely chopped

Pour boiling stock over the cornbread crumbs, mixing well. Add celery, onions, salt, pepper, sage and raw eggs. Mix well. Add chopped boiled eggs last. Bake with breasts of chicken, thighs or with a small chicken at 350° for 1½ hours. Serves 2 or 3.

Lucy Glee Fullingim
Odessa, Texas

BREAD DRESSING

1½ cups chopped celery
1½ cups chopped onions
1½ cups cornmeal
1½ cups flour
3 teaspoons baking powder
1 teaspoon salt
2 teaspoons sugar
⅓ cup butter
3 eggs
1½ cups milk

Mix all ingredients and bake like cornbread. This will freeze well. To make dressing: crumble up cornbread and pour broth over it; add 2 eggs and any seasoning you like.

Joy Keener
Sweeny, Texas

NOTES:

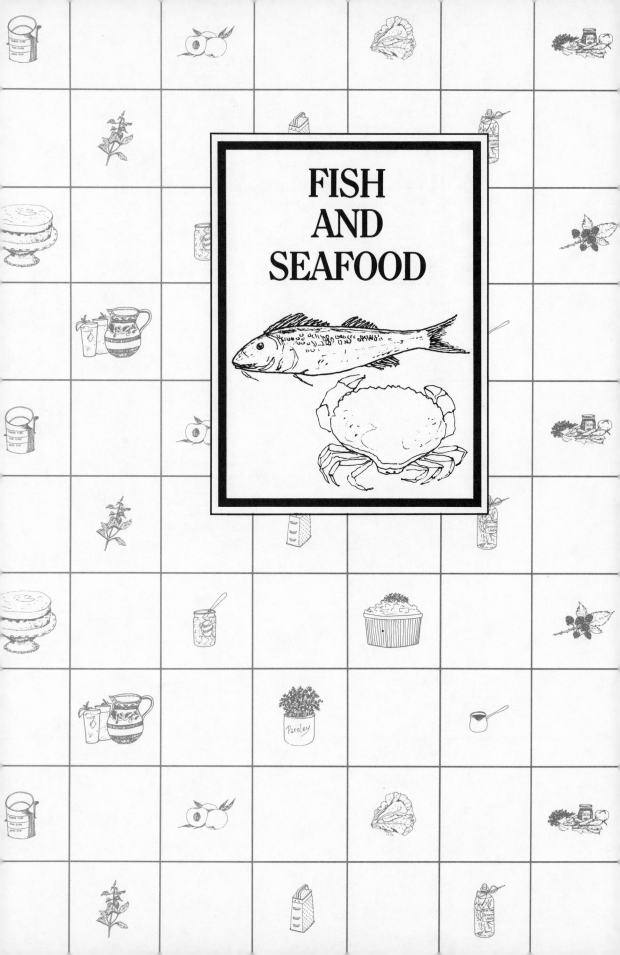

FISH
AND
SEAFOOD

ISLAND STUFFED FLOUNDER

1 large flounder
½ cup chopped celery
½ cup chopped onion
½ cup toasted bread crumbs
¾ cup crabmeat
Butter or margarine
Lemon juice

Cut flounder lengthwise down the middle and crosswise behind the gills and above the tail. Separate the fish from the bones with a knife, making "pockets" for stuffing. Mix celery, onion, bread crumbs and crabmeat, and put mixture in pockets and on top of the flounder. Add a few tablespoons of butter or margarine and lemon juice to the top, repeating the process twice during baking time. Bake uncovered at 375° for 1 hour or until the fish is white, light and flaky.

Lisa Farmer
Galveston, Texas

ROLLOVER PASS FISH ROLLS

1½ to 2 pounds fish fillets
1 teaspoon salt
1 teaspoon Accent
¼ teaspoon pepper
2½ tablespoons butter or margarine
1 tablespoon chopped onion
½ cup dry white wine
Additional tablespoon butter
2 tablespoons flour
½ cup heavy cream
Lemon wedges
White grapes

"My grandfather, Papaw, had a summer place at Gilchrist near Roll Over Pass. We always had lots of fish and seafood so I decided to send my best fish recipe."

Roll fillets and fasten with wooden picks. Season them with the salt, Accent and pepper. Set fish aside.

Heat electric skillet to low setting. Sauté onion in butter until tender. Place fish in skillet and add wine. Place lid tightly on skillet and cook about 10 minutes, or until fish flakes. Carefully remove to serving platter.

Reserve pan juices for sauce. Melt 1 tablespoon butter in a saucepan. Stir in 2 tablespoons flour. Gradually add fish juices and heavy cream. Cook about 1 to 2 minutes, until thickened and smooth. Spoon sauce over fish. Garnish with lemon wedges and white grapes.

Laura Alice Phipps
Mineral Wells, Texas

BAKED ORANGE ROUGHY IN HERBED BUTTER SAUCE

1½ to 2 pounds orange roughy fillets
1 stick butter
3 tablespoons soy sauce
1 teaspoon garlic powder
½ teaspoon basil
1 teaspoon oregano
¼ teaspoon thyme
½ teaspoon rosemary
¼ teaspoon tarragon
¼ cup sliced mushrooms
¼ cup chopped green onions
1 lemon, sliced

Lay fillets in baking dish. In small saucepan, melt butter; add soy sauce and herbs. Pour over fillets and bake at 375° for 8 minutes.

Remove from oven. Put mushrooms, onions and lemon slices on top of fish. Baste with sauce until mushrooms and onions are well coated. Return to oven and bake 5 minutes.

Mrs. F. Lynn Tankersley
Houston, Texas

CATFISH CREOLE

2 pounds fresh catfish, pan-dressed and skinned
1½ cups uncooked regular rice
1 medium onion, chopped
1 medium-sized green pepper, chopped
2 tablespoons vegetable oil
2 15-ounce cans tomato sauce with tomato bits
1 2-ounce jar diced pimientos, drained
1 tablespoon sugar
½ teaspoon salt
¼ teaspoon pepper

Place catfish in a large Dutch oven; cover with water. Bring to a boil, reduce heat, and simmer 10 minutes or until fish flakes easily when tested with a fork. Drain fish, reserving 3⅓ cups broth. Cool fish slightly; remove flesh from bone in large pieces. Set aside.

Bring reserved broth to a boil in medium saucepan; add rice; cover and simmer 20 minutes.

Sauté onion and green pepper in oil until tender. Add

tomato sauce, pimientos, sugar and seasonings; cover and simmer 10 minutes. Add catfish; cover and simmer 5 minutes. Serve over hot rice. Makes 6 servings.

Glenda Chastain
Channelview, Texas

POOR FOLK SALMON PATTIES

2 15-ounce cans salmon, well drained
3 medium to large potatoes, boiled and mashed
1 cup chopped onions
2 eggs, very well beaten
Salt and pepper
Oil
Lemon wedges

Combine first 5 ingredients. Make patties and fry in oil. Garnish with lemon wedges. Serve hot.

Mary Ellen Ledesma
Bertram, Texas

SHRIMP FIESTA

1 12-ounce can of beer
½ onion
1 sprig parsley
1 lemon wedge
1 bay leaf
1 teaspoon salt
2 pounds raw shrimp, peeled
2 tablespoons butter
2 tablespoons flour
1 8-ounce can tomato sauce
4 tablespoons chopped green onions
¼ tablespoon hot sauce
¼ teaspoon nutmeg
¼ teaspoon sugar

Bring beer, onion, parsley, lemon wedge, bay leaf and salt to boil in a large saucepan. Add shrimp and reduce heat. Simmer for 5 minutes. Strain liquid and reserve. Melt butter and add flour to blend. Add shrimp liquid, tomato sauce, green onion, hot sauce, nutmeg and sugar. Cook until thickened. Add shrimp and cook 3 minutes more. Serve with rice or hot buttered noodles.

Kathy Vignone
Santa Fe, Texas

SHRIMP GUMBO

"Since I originally came from the Cajun country of Lafayette, Louisiana, and enjoy Cajun cooking as a hobby, I thought your readers might enjoy trying this recipe."

The real heart of gumbo is the roux. This is the time-consuming task of making this dish. Roux is a mixture of cooking oil and flour. A heavy iron pot is best for making the roux.

1 cup cooking oil
1 cup flour

Heat the oil over medium heat and add the flour very slowly; stir constantly with a wooden spoon until roux is a medium brown. Be sure the heat is not high enough to turn the roux dark brown or scorch it. If you do burn it, you might as well start over.

The stirring time for making the roux is from 30 to 45 minutes. This is the main reason you can't compare real Cajun gumbo to the kind you might buy in a restaurant. There is no way to substitute for real roux.

4 stalks celery, chopped
2 medium onions, chopped
1 medium pod garlic, chopped
2 medium green peppers, chopped
4 pounds fresh cleaned shrimp
1 quart chicken broth (or stock)
1 quart water
¼ cup Worcestershire sauce
Salt and pepper to taste
Cayenne pepper to taste (it only takes a little)
1 or 2 bay leaves
⅛ teaspoon thyme
⅛ teaspoon rosemary
1 package sliced okra
Gumbo filé powder

Add celery, onion, garlic and green pepper to roux, and cook on a very low heat for approximately 35 minutes, stirring constantly. (This will make the gumbo better.) Add clean raw shrimp to roux mixture and cook 10 more minutes, stirring constantly. Add chicken broth and water, Worcestershire sauce, salt, pepper, cayenne pepper, bay leaves, thyme and rosemary. Simmer in covered pot for approximately 2½ hours. Add okra the last 30 minutes of simmering time. Just before serving add filé. Start with a tablespoon and add filé lightly, stirring the gumbo to your desired thickness. Put a generous amount of cooked rice in a soup bowl and spoon gumbo over rice. Serve at once.

Jim La Coste
Trinity, Texas

SHRIMP CASSEROLE

1 can cream of mushroom soup
2 tablespoons finely chopped green pepper
2 tablespoons finely chopped onion
2 tablespoons butter, melted
1 package wild rice mix, cooked as directed
½ teaspoon Worcestershire sauce
½ teaspoon dry mustard
½ cup grated cheddar cheese
1 16-ounce package shrimp, thawed
Salt and pepper to taste

Mix all ingredients. Cook in buttered casserole in 375° oven for 35 minutes. Serves 4 to 6. Excellent prepared beforehand or left-over.

Mrs. Jack Rook
Channelview, Texas

BARBECUED SHRIMP

1 large onion, chopped
1 small can tomato sauce
1 clove garlic, crushed
Salt and black pepper to taste
1 level teaspoon chili powder
1 level teaspoon Worcestershire sauce
1 pound large shrimp, unpeeled

Sauté the chopped onions in shallow cooking oil until nearly transparent. Add tomato sauce, garlic, salt, pepper, chili powder and Worcestershire sauce.

Stir constantly until the sauce has thickened well, about 15 minutes. Add shrimp and cook until done. (If shrimp are frozen, thaw with running cold water, not hot water, and drain well before cooking.)

R. W. Smith
Houston, Texas

SHRIMP BATTER

1 cup flour
½ teaspoon sugar
½ teaspoon salt
1 egg
1 cup ice water
2 tablespoons vegetable oil

Mix together all ingredients until smooth. Dip raw shrimp into batter and fry in hot oil.

Gloria R. Payette
San Leon, Texas

MAMOO'S SHRIMP AND CRAB GUMBO

1 cooked chicken fryer
3 quarts water
6 slices bacon
¼ cup flour
3 cups finely chopped onion
1 cup finely chopped celery
1 cup finely chopped bell pepper
3 tablespoons vinegar or lemon juice
2 tablespoons garlic powder
Worcestershire sauce
Tabasco sauce
Salt and pepper
10 ounces frozen okra or 2 tablespoons gumbo filé
3 tablespoons parsley
½ cup green-onion tops
3 pounds shrimp
1 6½-ounce can crabmeat, drained and rinsed

First, cook chicken in 1 quart water and use this broth as part of the water. When chicken has cooled, chop in bite-size pieces. Cut 6 slices bacon in small pieces, and cook in a large pan. Take bacon out; put in small bowl until later.

Add ¼ cup flour to the bacon drippings in pan. Cook over low heat, stirring constantly to make a brown roux (do not burn). Add onion, cooking until browned and soft. Add chopped celery and bell pepper. Stir well. Add vinegar or lemon juice, garlic powder, a few dashes of Worcestershire sauce and Tabasco sauce, and salt and pepper to taste. Add water and the bacon, and cook slowly about 45 minutes. Add the okra or gumbo filé. Then add the parsley and onion tops. Finally add the chopped chicken, shrimp and crabmeat. Cook on low for 15 minutes. Serve over rice.

Don and Miriam Kimball
Alvin, Texas

DEVILED CRAB

3 tablespoons flour
1 stick butter or margarine
1 small can evaporated milk, diluted with equal amount of
    water
1 tablespoon prepared mustard
1 large green pepper, chopped
1 clove garlic, chopped
4 sprigs parsley, chopped
3 green onions (use tops only)
1 pound crabmeat
Crushed cracker crumbs

"This is an old family recipe dating back over sixty-two years to when my mother, Mrs. J. F. Cooper, lived in Beaumont, Texas, as a bride. Mother enjoyed learning to cook the fresh seafood available in the Gulf Coast area."

Make a cream sauce of flour and ½ stick butter or margarine, using the milk-water mixture to thicken sauce, but do not brown. Add mustard and chopped pepper, garlic, parsley, onion tops, and crabmeat. Put in cleaned crab shells or ramekins. Cover with crushed cracker crumbs. Melt remainder of butter and pour over top of shells. Bake 30 minutes at 350°. Serves 4 to 6, depending on size of shells or serving dishes used.

Carolyn C. Grine
College Station, Texas

OYSTERS EN BROCHETTE A LA SAN LEON

1 stick butter
3 large cloves garlic (more if you like), mashed
2 quarts large fresh oysters
Salt
Black pepper
Tabasco sauce
Lemon
Cornmeal
Minced parsley
Bacon

Melt butter with fresh garlic in slow oven. Take pan out of oven and place oysters in pan (single layer only). Now sprinkle salt and pepper, 1 drop Tabasco sauce, squeeze of lemon juice, ½ teaspoon cornmeal and minced parsley individually on each oyster. Place a piece of bacon on top of each oyster. Place pan on lower shelf in oven and turn broiler on. Let cook until bacon is crisp and oysters are firm. Serve with crackers.

Gloria R. Payette
San Leon, Texas

CRAWFISH ETOUFFEE

½ cup oil
½ cup flour
¾ cup chopped bell pepper
1 cup chopped green onion
3 stems celery, chopped
½ cup chopped parsley
½ teaspoon Tony Chachere's Seasoning
1 teaspoon salt
Cayenne pepper to taste
2 pounds peeled raw crawfish tails
Fat from the crawfish heads or 1 can cream of celery soup

Make a roux by stirring oil and flour together over medium heat until light brown. Add vegetables to the roux cooking about 10 minutes. Add the crawfish tails and 3 cups of water, or enough to make it the consistency you desire. Cook at least 30 minutes on low. Adjust seasonings. Serve over rice.

Doyle Schaer
El Campo, Texas

CRAWFISH SAUCE PIQUANT

½ cup oil
½ cup flour
¾ cup chopped bell pepper
3 stems celery, chopped
1 cup chopped green onion
½ cup chopped parsley
2 pounds cleaned raw crawfish tails
1 48-ounce can V-8 juice
1 8-ounce can tomato sauce
½ cup chopped green olives
½ teaspoon salt
⅔ cup picante sauce

Make a roux by stirring oil and flour together over medium heat until light brown. Combine vegetables in the roux. Add the crawfish tails, V-8 juice, tomato sauce, olives, salt and picante sauce. Simmer on low for 30 minutes. Serve over rice.

Doyle Schaer
El Campo, Texas

CRAWFISH JAMBALAYA CASSEROLE

1 medium onion, chopped
¼ bell pepper, chopped
3 stems celery, chopped
½ cup oil
2 pounds crawfish tails, peeled
1 clove garlic
½ cup chopped green onions
1 8-ounce can tomato sauce
2½ to 3 cups water
1½ cup raw rice

Sauté onions, bell pepper and celery in oil. Add crawfish, garlic, green onions, tomato sauce, water and seasonings to taste. Cook about 10 minutes, then add rice and place in a 2½-quart covered casserole and bake at 350° for 1 hour or until rice is done.

Doyle Schaer
El Campo, Texas

SPICY SAUCE FOR FISH OR CHICKEN

Juice of ½ lemon or lime
⅛ cup olive oil
½ cup chopped onion
1 tablespoon chopped garlic
1 16-ounce can whole peeled tomatoes
½ can chopped green chilies
½ teaspoon salt
½ cup pimiento-stuffed olives, chopped
½ teaspoon oregano
⅛ cup capers
⅛ teaspoon hot pepper sauce

Sprinkle juice on 1 to 2 pounds of fish or chicken. In large skillet, heat oil and add onion to sauté. Next, add garlic and sauté about 1 minute. Drain tomatoes, reserving juice, and add to skillet, breaking up tomatoes with a spoon. Add remaining ingredients. Bring to a boil, reduce heat, and cook 10 minutes uncovered. Pour sauce over fish arranged in a glass baking dish. Bake in oven at 350° for 45 minutes uncovered. If sauce gets too thick, add reserved juice from tomatoes.

Nita Rivoire
Sugar Land, Texas

WILBUR'S REMOULADE SAUCE

3 heaping tablespoons mayonnaise
3 tablespoons Worcestershire sauce
1 tablespoon black pepper

The above amounts are approximate. Adjust to suit your own taste.

R. W. Smith
Houston, Texas

TEX-MEX DISHES

TEX-MEX DIP

1 package taco seasoning mix
1 cup sour cream
½ cup mayonnaise
3 medium-ripe avocados
2 tablespoons lemon juice
½ teaspoon salt
¼ teaspoon pepper
2 cans plain or jalapeño bean dip
1 large bunch green onions and tops, chopped
3 medium-size tomatoes, coarsely chopped
1 large can ripe pitted olives, coarsely chopped
½ pound sharp cheddar cheese, grated

Mix together taco seasoning with sour cream and mayonnaise. Mix avocados with lemon juice, salt and pepper. Layer everything starting with bean dip and ending with cheese. Serve with large round tortilla chips.

Marjorie McIntosh
Houston, Texas

TORTILLA SOUP

6 green onions, chopped
3 medium tomatoes, peeled and chopped
3 ribs celery, chopped
1 tablespoon chopped green chilies
½ green pepper, chopped
2 tablespoons vegetable oil
6 corn tortillas, cut in half
Additional vegetable oil
4½ cups chicken broth
1 bay leaf, crushed
Cilantro to taste
Salt and pepper
Cheddar cheese, shredded

Sauté onions, tomatoes, celery, green chilies and bell pepper in 2 tablespoons oil until soft. Remove with slotted spoon. Fry tortilla pieces in oil until crisp. Drain and set aside. Bring broth to boil, add vegetables, tortilla pieces, bay leaf and cilantro. Simmer, covered, for 30 minutes. Add salt and pepper. Serve with grated cheese. Serves 6. Freezes well.

Lynda Kapalski
Dayton, Texas

SOPA DE ELOTE (MEXICAN CORN SOUP)

2 15-ounce cans whole-kernel corn
2 tablespoons butter
1 small onion, chopped
1 clove garlic, crushed
1 large can (about 24 ounces) whole tomatoes, chopped
½ teaspoon salt
1 quart beef broth
½ teaspoon dried oregano
¼ cup whipping cream
Cilantro or parsley leaves, optional

Drain liquid from canned corn. Puree corn in a blender or food processor; set aside. Melt butter in a large saucepan and add onions and garlic. Cook until onion is tender but not browned. Add tomatoes and salt. Cook slowly about 10 minutes, mashing tomatoes with a spoon. Add broth, oregano and pureed corn. Bring to a boil, then reduce heat. Cover and simmer 30 minutes. Stir in whipping cream. Garnish with cilantro or parsley, if desired. Makes 6 servings.

Connie Henderson
Austin, Texas

TEX-MEX BLACK BEAN SOUP

2 pounds black beans, washed and sorted
Large ham bone with meat, or ham hocks
3 or 4 large onions, chopped fine
7 or 8 ribs chopped celery and leaves
Parsley, chopped
6 large cloves garlic, chopped
4 bay leaves
1 or 2 teaspoons ground thyme
1 or 2 teaspoons oregano
1 teaspoon ground cumin
Garlic and onion salt to taste
Red pepper to taste
1 cup hot picante sauce
1 cup Madeira wine

Cover all ingredients with water in a large pot, except picante sauce and wine. Cook several hours or overnight in slow cooker until beans are tender. Remove bones and bay leaves. Leave in hunks of ham. Stir in picante sauce (more if you desire) and Madeira wine. Serve immediately.

Gayle Yoder
Seabrook, Texas

TACO SOUP

1½ pounds ground beef
1 medium onion, chopped
1 envelope taco seasoning
1 can hominy
1 can Trappey's pinto beans
1 envelope of ranch-style salad dressing
3 cans of tomatoes (stewed are the best)
Grated cheese (optional)

Brown the meat and chopped onion. Add the remaining ingredients (except cheese) to the meat and onion. Bring all 7 ingredients to a boil and simmer for 45 minutes or 1 hour. Serves 12. Prior to serving you may sprinkle each bowlful with grated cheese.

   Note: Do not drain any of the ingredients except ground beef that is not extra lean.

Jennifer Hill, age 11
East Bernard, Texas

AVOCADO SALAD

Juice of 1 lemon
2 large ripe avocados, peeled and mashed
1 large tomato, coarsely chopped
1 medium onion, chopped medium fine
1 4-ounce can chopped green chilies
Salt and pepper to taste

Combine all ingredients and serve with tortilla chips.

Ruby Schafer
Houston, Texas

TACO SALAD

1½ pounds ground meat
1 onion, chopped
Salt and pepper
½ head lettuce, shredded
1 tomato, cubed
1 avocado, cubed
1 8-ounce package macaroni, cooked
1 package taco-flavored Doritos, crumbled
1 8-ounce bottle thousand island dressing

Brown meat with onion, adding salt and pepper to taste. Drain fat from meat and mix with other ingredients.

Mrs. J. P. Pfieffer
Bastrop, Texas

MEXICAN SALAD

1½ pounds ground chuck
1 onion, chopped
1 bell pepper, chopped
1 package taco seasoning
4 tablespoons chili powder
1 No. 300 can pinto beans
1 can Campbell's Cheddar Cheese soup
½ head lettuce, chopped
3 tomatoes, diced
1 package tortilla chips
1 pound cheddar cheese, grated

Brown ground chuck, onions and bell pepper with taco seasoning and chili powder; add beans and cheddar cheese soup and simmer a few minutes.

To serve, place a mound of lettuce with tomatoes on an ovenproof plate. Top with tortilla chips, cover with sauce and sprinkle with grated cheese. To melt cheese, place under broiler. Take out and serve. For added flavor, top with guacamole and sour cream.

Larry Maynard
Crosby, Texas

CHORIZO

2 or 3 cloves garlic
1 pound ground pork
½ pound ground chuck
½ teaspoon each oregano and cumin
2 tablespoons chili powder
1 teaspoon salt
½ teaspoon vinegar
Few drops lemon juice

Mash and mince garlic, then add to meat with spices, vinegar and lemon juice. Mix well. Let chorizo ripen in refrigerator at least 24 hours.

Cook small amount of chorizo in skillet for about 10 minutes, stirring every now and then. Add about 3 eggs and scramble with the meat. Serve with tortillas. Chorizo is also good for seasoning pinto beans.

Gloria Rose Payette
Livingston, Texas

ROPA VIEJA
(Old Clothes)

1 5-ounce jar dried beef
2 tablespoons butter or margarine
2 tablespoons flour
1 3-ounce jar sliced mushrooms, drained
1 clove garlic, minced
1 cup meat broth
½ cup dry wine
Chopped parsley or cilantro
Hot, cooked rice

Cover dried beef with boiling water to remove some of the salt; drain and pull in shreds (to resemble rags). Brown butter and flour in saucepan. Add mushrooms and garlic and sauté 2 to 3 minutes. Add broth and wine and cook, stirring until thickened. Add dried beef and simmer gently about 15 minutes. Garnish with parsley or cilantro. Serve on rice.

Mary Ellen Ledesma
Bertram, Texas

FAJITAS, TEXAS STYLE

3 pounds skirt steak, cut about ½-inch thick
1 recipe marinade (see below)

Marinate meat overnight, turning once. Build a hot fire, then spread out the coals after they are glowing well. Put marinated meat on grill in a single layer. The oil from the marinade will cause the fire to flare up initially. This can be extinguished by closing the lid on the barbecue pit. Cook meat approximately 30 minutes, turning every 7 or 8 minutes. Slice crossways into strips ½-inch wide. Serve with warm flour tortillas, *pico de gallo,* and hot sauce. Spanish rice makes a nice accompaniment. [These recipes appear elsewhere in this section.]

FAJITAS MARINADE:
¼ cup lemon juice
¾ cup salad oil
½ cup soy sauce
¼ cup Worcestershire sauce
2 or 3 garlic cloves, chopped

Mix ingredients together and pour over meat. Cover and refrigerate.

Earl W. Olson
Houston, Texas

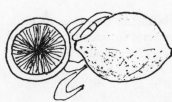

PICADILLO I

1 pound lean ground beef
1 large onion, coarsely chopped
1 16-ounce can tomatoes, undrained
2 tablespoons vinegar
1 teaspoon cinnamon
Pinch of ground cloves
¼ teaspoon ground cumin
1 teaspoon chili powder
½ cup white raisins
1 4-ounce can chopped green chilies
1 cup frozen whole kernel corn, plus ¼ cup water
½ cup chopped peanuts (optional)
1 cup grated sharp cheddar cheese

Brown beef. Add onion and sauté until onion begins to soften. Pour off excess fat. Add tomatoes and break them up. Add vinegar, cinnamon, cloves, cumin, chili powder, raisins, green chilies and corn. Heat to boiling; reduce heat and simmer 10 minutes. Stir in peanuts and sprinkle with cheese. Cover and cook over very low heat about 10 minutes or until cheese is melted. Makes 4 to 6 servings.

Serve over tortilla chips and top with shredded lettuce. Very good served with the following Avocado Salad.

Ruby Schafer
Houston, Texas

PICADILLO II

3 cups water
1 pound stew beef, cut into cubes
2 teaspoons oil
¾ cup chopped onion
2 cloves garlic, minced
2 tablespoons raisins
8 small pimiento-stuffed olives, sliced
½ teaspoon allspice
½ teaspoon salt
¼ teaspoon cinnamon
⅛ teaspoon cayenne pepper

In medium saucepan, bring water to boil over medium high heat. Add the beef, cover and simmer 1½ hours, or until the beef is tender. Shred the beef and reserve ½ cup of the broth.

In a large nonstick skillet, heat the oil over medium

heat. Add the onion and the garlic and sauté until the onion is transparent. Stir in the remaining ingredients and the reserved beef and broth. Simmer, uncovered, until sauce thickens.

Mrs. William McNamara
Dime Box, Texas

TEX-MEX CHILI

"With this recipe that I have evolved and developed over the past 15 years, I have won three first places, four seconds and numerous other awards in chili cook-offs I have entered."

4 *pounds chuck roast* (you can use blade roast or any good-quality but less expensive cut of meat. You may also use venison or other wild game meat, even bear)
1 *pound coarsely ground pork*

Cut roast into 1- to 1½-inch cubes, including fat. Do not trim. Use a heavy deep pot, and place *1 cup of vegetable oil* in pot on stove and place cubed roast and ground pork in pot. You can try doing this in your fireplace if you have the pioneer spirit, but I would recommend the more conventional stove-top method for the first time. Turn on the burner and stir until all the meat is completely grayish in color. During this cooking process, chop *2 medium white onions* and put them in with the meat to begin cooking.

In a small mixing bowl, combine the following and set aside:
2 *heaping teaspoons dried minced onions*
4 *teaspoons salt*
3 *teaspoons paprika*
1 *teaspoon red pepper (cayenne, if available)*
2 *tablespoons ground cumin*
12 *tablespoons chili powder (the fresher the better)*

Add to meat mixture the following:
2 *8-ounce cans tomato sauce*
32 *ounces water (1 quart)*
Spice mixture (above)

Stir well and bring to a simmer while stirring. Simmer slowly for 2 to 2½ hours, stirring occasionally, until meat is tender. Place off the burner for 15 minutes, which will allow grease to rise to the top. Skim off the grease and discard it.

In a small cup, mix *2 tablespoons masa flour* with a small amount of warm water until about the consistency of thick cream. Place the chili back on burner and bring to a simmer again. Stir in the masa mixture while constantly stirring. Simmer about another 15 to 30 minutes, stirring occasionally. Test for meat tenderness and add more salt if desired.

During simmering of chili, you may find it thickening up too much. If so, do not hesitate to add water to thin it down.

If beans are desired, cook pinto or red beans separately and add to the bowls after dipping chili. Do not place beans in chili pot. Leftover chili can be frozen for later use, but there is usually none left to freeze. Before serving, add a cold bottle of beer, crisp crackers, a cold winter day (sleeting or snowing if possible) and a warm fire.

Tom Wiseheart
Houston, Texas

TEXAS-STYLE CHILI

1 green pepper, chopped
2 onions, chopped
1 large stalk celery, chopped
1 fresh jalapeño pepper, seeds removed and chopped
1 clove garlic, minced
4 tablespoons oil
3 pounds chili meat
¼ teaspoon Tabasco
2 teaspoons garlic salt
1 tablespoon cumin
¼ cup Mexican chili powder
⅛ teaspoon black pepper
1 bottle Texas beer (not light beer)
1 14-ounce can whole tomatoes
1 6-ounce can tomato paste
1 8-ounce can tomato sauce
1¼ cups water
1 4-ounce can chopped green chilies, drained
2 15-ounce cans ranch style beans, drained and rinsed

Sauté the first 5 ingredients in the oil until the onions are clear. Add the chili meat and cook until browned. Drain. Add Tabasco, garlic salt, cumin, Mexican chili powder, black pepper and 8 ounces of beer (the other 4 ounces is for the cook). Let stand for 2 minutes. Add tomatoes, tomato paste, tomato sauce, water and green chilies. Simmer for 3 hours. Add the beans during the last 30 minutes of cooking. Serve with corn chips.

Dayna Hayes
Odessa, Texas

ANYBODY-CAN-EAT-IT CHILI

3 pounds ground beef
1½ large onions, chopped
1½ bell peppers, chopped
¼ teaspoon chopped garlic
1 tomato, chopped
3 ounces Worcestershire sauce
1 tablespoon salt
3 tablespoons black pepper
½ teaspoon cayenne pepper
2 tablespoons Cajun creole seasoning
1 tablespoon Mrs. Dash's seasoning
1 teaspoon Accent

"My husband made this chili for supper the other night by just putting this and that into the pot. It was so good, he decided to write up a recipe. The second pot of chili was even better."

Judy Heintschel

Mix all of the above ingredients in a large pot, brown meat on high until done, stirring occasionally. Then add:
4 tablespoons picante sauce
1 8-ounce can tomato sauce
½ cup ketchup
1 jalapeño (optional)
1 tablespoon honey
1 ounce beer (optional)
4 cups water

Simmer for approximately 1 hour.

Gerald Heintschel
Columbus, Texas

MY FAMILY'S FAVORITE CHILI

2 pounds ground chuck
1 large onion, chopped
2 cloves garlic, minced, or 2 teaspoons garlic powder
1 8-ounce can tomato sauce
1 package chili seasoning mix
1½ teaspoons cumin powder
1 10-ounce can Rotel tomatoes with chilies
1 15-ounce can kidney or pinto beans (optional)
2 cups hot water

Sauté meat, onions and garlic in a heavy pot. Cook 4 to 5 minutes. Drain off excess fat. Add remaining ingredients and blend well. Bring to a boil and then reduce heat and simmer for 1 hour. Add more water if needed during cooking. Chili may be served at once but is better if set aside for a while before serving. Serves 4 to 6.

Louise Kowis
Livingston, Texas

PAT'S CHILI POT

1½ pounds ground beef, browned and drained
1½ tablespoons chili powder
1 16-ounce can tomatoes
2 cups pinto beans
1 clove garlic, minced
1 onion, chopped
1 16-ounce can whole kernel corn

Combine above ingredients and cook on low heat for 2 hours. Serve in casserole topped with grated colby cheese.

Pat Bostick
La Marque, Texas

VENISON CHILI

2 pounds venison chili meat
1 tablespoon (or more) chili powder
Salt and black pepper to taste
1 46-ounce can V-8 juice
1 large onion, diced
1 large clove garlic, minced
2 medium-size potatoes, diced
1 No. 2 can ranch style beans

In large pot, brown chili meat. While browning, add chili powder, salt and pepper. After browned, add V-8 juice, onions, garlic and potatoes. Bring to boil, lower heat and let simmer till meat is tender. Add beans and heat through.

Serve with crackers or hot rolls and cheese and celery sticks.

Leftover chili is good for making Frito Pie. Pour heated chili over Fritos, top with diced tomatoes, pickles, olives, cheese or whatever you like.

Virginia A. Helweg
Shiner, Texas

MEXICAN LASAGNA

1 10-ounce package cheddar cheese
1 10-ounce package Monterey jack cheese
1 10-ounce package Swiss cheese
1 can cream of mushroom soup
1 can cream of celery soup
1 can cream of chicken soup
1 16-ounce carton sour cream
16 ounces cream cheese, softened
1 package taco seasoning mix

1 small jar diced pimientos
1 large jar sliced mushrooms
1 large can black olives, sliced
Jalapeño slices (to desired heat)
1 chicken, cooked and deboned
20 to 30 large flour tortillas

Shred cheeses and set aside. Mix undiluted soups, sour cream, cream cheese, taco seasoning mix, pimientos, mushrooms, black olives and peppers. Bring to low boil. Remove from heat and add chicken.

Butter sides and bottom of 4- to 6-quart dutch oven. Beginning with the flour tortillas, start to alternate tortillas, mixture and cheese. End with cheese on top. Cook at 350° for 30 minutes (uncovered). Allow to stand for 15 minutes before serving (covered).

Serve with tossed salad. Yields 6–8 servings.

Rachel Nash
Shepherd, Texas

ENCHILADA CASSEROLE

2 pounds ground chuck
1 can cream of mushroom soup, undiluted
1 can cream of chicken soup, undiluted
1½ cans enchilada sauce
1 large onion, chopped
6 or 8 regular-size corn tortillas (tear into quarters)
10 ounces grated cheddar cheese

Brown meat lightly and add soups and enchilada sauce; simmer about 15 minutes. Lightly sauté chopped onion and add to meat mixture.

Layer ingredients in a medium-size casserole, starting with meat sauce, then corn tortillas. Make about 3 layers, ending with tortillas soaked in sauce. Bake until bubbly, then add grated cheese and return to oven or microwave until cheese melts.

If preparing for the freezer, omit the cheese until ready to heat and serve.

Mrs. Hershel Orr
West Columbia, Texas

ENCHILADAS

Mix together in saucepan:
5 tablespoons flour
5 tablespoons chili powder (mild)
2 teaspoons salt
½ teaspoon ground cumin
6 cloves garlic, crushed
3 cups water

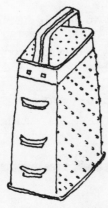

Blend all dry ingredients. Mix with garlic and water until well blended, then cook, stirring until thickened, about 10 minutes.

Dip tortillas in hot oil for a few seconds then in sauce, then fill and roll up. Fillings can be one of the following:
Cheese and onion
Cooked ground meat with garlic and onion and some of the sauce
Boiled, boned, shredded chicken with some of the sauce

Gloria Rose Payette
Livingston, Texas

ENCHILADAS WITH GOAT CHEESE AND BLACK BEANS

2 cups black beans, mashed or refried (set aside)

To make sauce:
3 large cloves garlic, crushed
2 large onions, chopped
¼ cup corn oil
2 14- or 15-ounce cans stewed tomatoes, chopped
1 bunch fresh cilantro (save some for garnish)
Salt and pepper to taste

In skillet, sauté garlic and onions in oil until slightly browned. Add tomatoes and simmer. Add fresh cilantro, cover and set aside.

2 cups goat cheese, crumbled (or substitute farmer's or mozzarella cheese)
Corn oil
12 to 18 white corn tortillas
Cilantro

To assemble: In skillet, heat about ½ cup corn oil. Very quickly dip tortillas in oil for approximately 5 seconds, then place in flat baking dish. Spoon some cheese and black beans into each tortilla, rolling with seam side down. Repeat with all tortillas, arranging in dish.

Spoon tomato sauce on generously. Bake 30 minutes in a 350° oven. Garnish with cilantro. Serve with a little side dish of hot sauce.

Mary Ellen Ledesma
Bertram, Texas

GREEN ENCHILADAS, TEXAS STYLE

2 pounds ground meat
½ cup onion, chopped
⅓ cup canned milk
1¼ pounds Velveeta cheese
1 can cream of mushroom soup, undiluted
1 can cream of chicken soup, undiluted
1 can green chilies, chopped
1 small jar pimientos
1 large package cheese-flavored Doritos
Grated cheddar

Brown meat with onion and set aside. Combine milk, Velveeta and soups, and warm. Stir constantly, as mixture sticks easily. Add chilies and pimientos. Use a 10×13-inch oiled casserole dish, and layer Doritos, meat and sauce. This will generally make 2 layers. Grate cheddar cheese on top and heat until cheese is melted.

Martha Dolan
Big Lake, Texas

MOCK ENCHILADAS

1 can white hominy
1 can chili without beans
8 ounces cheddar or Monterey jack cheese, grated

In baking dish, layer hominy, chili and cheese. Repeat process. Bake at 325° for 30 minutes.

Crispina Babbitt
Austin, Texas

CHICKEN TORTILLA CASSEROLE

3 cups cooked chicken, cut into bite-sized pieces
1 onion, chopped
1 4-ounce can chopped green chilies, drained
1 cup milk
1 can cream of chicken soup, undiluted
1 can cream of mushroom soup, undiluted
2 tablespoons margarine
12 small flour tortillas, quartered
1 pound grated American cheese

Combine chicken, onion, green chilies, milk and soups and set aside. Melt margarine in a 9×13-inch pan and coat bottom. Layer bottom of pan with flour tortilla quarters, chicken mixture and cheese. Repeat, ending with cheese on top. Refrigerate overnight. Bake in a pre-heated 350° oven for 1 hour or until hot and bubbly. This freezes well.

Dayna Hayes
Odessa, Texas

AÑA'S FABULOUS HAM TACOS

These tacos have unique flavor and complement any traditional Mexican cuisine.

16 ounces coarsely ground cooked picnic ham
1 large sweet white onion, grated
2 cloves fresh garlic, pressed or minced
Chopped cilantro
1 teaspoon ground cumin
12 corn tortillas—extra thick
Oil for frying—preferably peanut
Chopped tomatoes
Shredded lettuce
Sour cream
2 cups grated sharp cheddar cheese
Salsa or Tabasco sauce

Mix ham, onion, garlic, cilantro and cumin together in a large bowl. Soften tortillas in oil and layer between paper towels. Heat oil in large skillet to 450°. Fill each tortilla with a tablespoon or more of the ham mixture and fold together. Hold the edges of the taco together with tongs and fry the bottom edge until it stays curved. Lay the taco on its side and fry until crisp, about 3 minutes. Turn the taco over and repeat the process. Drain tacos on paper towels on large platter. While the cooking process continues, place the prepared tacos in a warm (200°) oven to keep them crisp.

Offer chopped tomatoes, shredded lettuce, sour cream, cheese and salsa as condiments. Refried beans and guacamole create a satisfying and nutritious Mexican dinner. Serves 6.

Anne Thorpe
Houston, Texas

TAMALE PIE

CORNMEAL CRUST:
1 cup yellow cornmeal
1 cup cold water
1 teaspoon salt
3 cups boiling water
2 tablespoons butter or margarine

FILLING:
2 tablespoons vegetable oil
½ cup chopped onion
½ cup chopped green pepper
1 pound lean ground beef
1 can whole tomatoes
1 can tomato paste
2 teaspoons chili powder
1 tablespoon salt
Pepper to taste
1 10-ounce package frozen cut corn
1 cup whole pitted black olives
½ cup shredded cheddar cheese

To make crust, combine cornmeal, cold water and salt, mixing until smooth. Put into boiling water in saucepan, stirring constantly until very thick. Cook about 10 minutes. Pour into a buttered shallow 2-quart casserole; let cool until mixture begins to stiffen, then spread evenly over bottom and sides of dish.

To make filling, heat oil in skillet and add onion and green pepper; sauté until tender. Add beef and cook until browned. Mix in tomatoes, tomato paste, chili powder, salt and pepper. Simmer 10 minutes; stir in corn and olives. Pour into cornmeal crust. Sprinkle top with cheese. Bake at 350° for 40 to 50 minutes.

Patricia Buckley
Friendswood, Texas

COWBOY TAMALE CHICKEN

½ cup grits
2 ½ cups boiling water
1 pound ground beef
1 tablespoon oil
1 package chili seasoning mix
Salt
Cayenne pepper
1 frying chicken, whole
Honey
Chili powder

"Out on the range, cowboys ate their wild turkeys stuffed with tamales. You might not have a wild turkey, but you can stuff a chicken."

To make a tamale-like filling, add grits to boiling water and simmer covered until thick. Brown meat in oil; stir in seasoning mix. Combine ground meat and grits. Add salt and cayenne to taste.

Stuff chicken with filling. Rub chicken with honey and sprinkle with chili powder. Bake covered at 350° for 1¼ hours or until tender

Fran Ammons
Missouri City, Texas

SOPA

1 package corn or flour tortillas
Chicken broth
1 can cream of mushroom soup
1 can cream of chicken soup
¼ cup jalapeño peppers or green chilies, chopped
1 medium onion, chopped
3 or 4 cups cooked chicken, boned and chopped
1 small can evaporated milk
1 pound sharp cheddar cheese, grated
Paprika to taste

Soften tortillas in hot chicken broth. While they are softening, combine the 2 soups, peppers, onions, chicken and evaporated milk. Bring to a boil.

Line a 9×13-inch casserole with a layer of softened tortillas, then a layer of half of the chicken mixture, then a layer of the cheese. Repeat the layers in that order. Top with paprika, then bake in preheated oven at 350° for 20 minutes or until bubbly.

Crispina Babbitt
Austin, Texas

MOLE CON GALLINA

2 small fryers, about 2 pounds each
2 medium onions, finely chopped
3 cloves garlic, pressed
Salt to taste
1 tablespoon ground coriander
1/2 teaspoon cinnamon
1/2 teaspoon cayenne pepper
1 3/4 cups water
2 medium tomatoes, peeled and seeded
1 teaspoon vinegar
1 bay leaf, crumbled
Cornstarch for thickening
4 tablespoons cooking oil
6 to 8 tablespoons chili powder
1/2 cup finely ground peanuts
2 ounces unsweetened chocolate
5 tablespoons toasted sesame seeds

Cut up chicken into serving pieces. Put in a pot with onions, garlic, salt, seasonings and water, and cook about 20 minutes. Blend tomatoes, vinegar, bay leaf and cornstarch until smooth. In another large pot, put oil and chili powder and let fry very gently. Take broth from chicken and pour into hot oil slowly, stirring quickly and adding ground peanuts, chocolate and sesame seeds; keep stirring until very smooth. Add chicken, cover and simmer about 15 minutes.

Mary Ellen Ledesma
Bertram, Texas

TÍO JUAN'S SPICY FOIL-BAKED BIRD

1 large Cornish game hen, or small chicken fryer, cut in half
Salt
Lemon pepper
4 tablespoons picante sauce
2 tablespoons dry white wine
1 tablespoon butter or margarine, melted
1 or 2 cloves garlic, minced
1 teaspoon chopped cilantro

Preheat oven to 350°. Season bird to your taste with salt and lemon pepper. Place each bird-half on a separate sheet of foil, skin side up. Top with mixture of picante, wine, melted butter, garlic and cilantro. Fold foil over, sealing tightly. Arrange in baking pan or dish. Bake 30 to 35 minutes (for Cornish hen) or 45 to 50 minutes (for chicken fryer). When done, transfer bird halves to serving platter. Pour juices into small saucepan and boil over high heat about 1 to 1½ minutes. Pour over birds and serve immediately.

Note: May be adapted for other game birds, such as quail and pheasant. Also, purists who cook only "from scratch" may make their own substitute for picante by chopping fresh tomato, jalapeño pepper and onion in proportions as desired.

John K. Gresham
Richmond, Texas

MIGAS

5 corn tortillas
¼ cup butter
5 eggs
Salt to taste
1 4-ounce can tomatoes and green chilies

Tear tortillas into bite-size bits. Melt butter in skillet and drop in tortilla bits. Stir, being sure to coat all bits with butter, and let them soft-fry. Whip eggs in a small bowl and pour over tortilla bits, stirring to scramble. Add salt to taste. In blender, combine tomatoes and green chilies until smooth; serve over migas.

Mary Ellen Ledesma
Bertram, Texas

SPANISH RICE

½ stick butter
½ large onion, chopped
1½ cups raw rice
1 8-ounce can tomato sauce
½ 10-ounce can Renown diced tomatoes and jalapeño chilies
  with cilantro
Water to make 3 cups of liquid
1½ teaspoons salt

Melt butter in a heavy saucepan. Cook onion in butter. Add rice and cook over low fire until slightly transparent. Mix together tomato sauce, tomatoes and chilies, water and salt. Add to onion and rice mixture. Bring this to a boil. Turn heat to low; cover. Cook 20 minutes, stirring once after about 10 minutes. Serve.

Earl W. Olson
Houston, Texas

NOPALITOS

3 *cups diced nopalitos (young pods of prickly pear cactus)*
1 large onion, chopped
½ cup cooking oil
3 cloves garlic, minced
1 tablespoon chili powder
½ cup cilantro, chopped
Salt to taste

After cleaning the nopalitos, rinse well, and dice or chop into cubes no larger than ½ inch. Boil 5 to 10 minutes in a pot of water. Remove from heat and pour into colander, rinsing well; put aside. In a skillet, sauté onions in oil until they are clear. Add garlic. Turn up heat to medium-high, then add nopalitos and chili powder. Cover and cook for 5 minutes. Mix in cilantro and serve. Salt to taste. This mixture can be used in omelets.

If using fresh cactus, use fresh leaves which come out in the spring. Carefully cut off the new leaves and remove the thorns, using a very sharp knife or a potato peeler. Clean and rinse well.

Mary Ellen Ledesma
Bertram, Texas

BAKED CHILES RELLENOS

1 can whole green chili peppers
½ pound sharp cheddar cheese
2 eggs
1½ cups milk
½ cup flour
1 teaspoon salt

Cut peppers lengthwise and place halves in bottom of buttered casserole. Cut cheese into finger-size pieces and put on top of chilies. Beat eggs slightly, adding milk, flour, salt; pour over cheese. Bake at 350° for 45 to 50 minutes.

If you need to double this recipe, bake in 2 dishes or allow lots of extra baking time for the center to set.

Jean Edwards
Austin, Texas

FLOUR TORTILLAS

3 cups flour
1½ teaspoons salt
2 teaspoons baking powder
2 rounded tablespoons lard
Warm water

Mix dry ingredients. Cut lard into flour. Add some warm water, a little at a time, and knead until dough is workable and does not stick to bowl. Pull off pieces of dough, shape into balls and roll out on floured board. Cook on hot griddle. They are cooked when they are well spotted with light brown. Serve hot with butter.

Gloria Rose Payette
Livingston, Texas

HOT PICANTE SAUCE

3 quarts peeled and quartered tomatoes
2 to 3 large onions, chopped fine
1 cup chopped jalapeño peppers
1 cup vinegar
⅓ cup sugar
1 tablespoon salt
4 cloves garlic, chopped

Mix all ingredients in a large pan and simmer 2 to 2½ hours, stirring occasionally and being careful not to let mixture stick. Pour into hot, sterile jars and seal with lids and rings. Process in hot-water bath 10 minutes. Makes 6 pints. Be sure to wear gloves when chopping jalapeño peppers. This will be hot or mild, depending on your peppers.

Debra Ramsden
Huffman, Texas

PICANTE SAUCE

1 16-ounce can tomatoes
2 cloves garlic
½ cup chopped onion
¼ to ½ bunch cilantro
2 to 4 jalapeños, seeded
½ teaspoon salt
1 teaspoon olive or cooking oil

Mix all in blender. Refrigerate.

Betty Lou Warren
Texas City, Texas

HOT SAUCE

1 16-ounce can whole tomatoes
1 16-ounce can stewed tomatoes
4 tablespoons salad oil
20 fresh jalapeño peppers with seeds and membranes
   removed
2 medium onions
2 teaspoons garlic powder
2 teaspoons garlic salt
2 teaspoons salt

Put ingredients in a blender (you may need to make 2 batches if you have a small blender). Process until pureed. Put in a saucepan and bring to a boil. Simmer 10 minutes. Put in sterilized jars and refrigerate until used.
   Note: If you want the sauce very hot, leave in the pepper seeds and membranes; if you want a mild sauce, add a clove or two of fresh garlic to tone down the peppers. Be sure to wear gloves when cleaning and seeding peppers.

Earl W. Olson
Houston, Texas

PICO DE GALLO

3 medium tomatillos (small green Mexican tomatoes)
3 medium red tomatoes
3 green onions
Fresh cilantro to taste

Chop the tomatillos, tomatoes and onions. Tear cilantro into small bits. Mix well and chill.

Earl W. Olson
Houston, Texas

SALSA FRESCA

4 tomatoes, peeled and chopped, with all liquid
1 onion, chopped
2 or more cloves garlic, minced very fine
½ bunch cilantro
1 jalapeño, seeded and minced
1 or 2 chiles serranos, seeded and minced
Juice of 1 or 2 limes

In a medium bowl, combine all the ingredients. Stir well, and chill about 2 hours to let flavors blend.

Connie Henderson
Austin, Texas

NOTES:

VEGETABLES

HOT ARTICHOKE PIE

1 cup mayonnaise
¾ cup Parmesan cheese, grated
1 6-ounce jar marinated artichoke hearts, drained and
    quartered

Combine all ingredients and place in 9-inch pie plate. Bake at 350° for 10 to 15 minutes. Best served with party rye bread.

Irene Bornet
Houston, Texas

BAKED BEANS I

1 onion, chopped
2 15-ounce cans pork and beans
1 teaspoon prepared mustard
½ cup vinegar
½ cup sugar
½ cup brown sugar
½ cup molasses
2 slices bacon

Add chopped onion to beans. Mix the mustard, vinegar and sugars. Pour into the beans. Put mixture in a baking dish. Pour molasses on the top. Lay the slices of bacon on top of the beans. Bake at 325° for 2½ to 3 hours.

Susan Grisbee
Austin, Texas

BAKED BEANS II

Brown the following:
2 tablespoons margarine
1 pound ground meat

In a large pan mix the following:
1 package onion soup mix
½ cup water
1 cup ketchup
1 tablespoon prepared mustard
1 teaspoon cider vinegar
2 1-pound-12-ounce cans pork and beans

Add browned meat to mixture. Bake 45 minutes to 1 hour at 325° to 350°.

Bobbie Dykes
Bay City, Texas

BAKED BEANS III

1 pound navy beans
1 medium onion
½ pound chunk bacon or salt pork
⅓ cup brown sugar
1 teaspoon salt
⅛ teaspoon black pepper
1 teaspoon dry mustard
½ cup molasses or cane syrup

Sort through beans, wash and soak in cold water overnight. In the morning, drain beans. Place onion, cut into 8ths, into bottom of crock bean pot or deep casserole with a cover. Put half of the bacon chunks over the onions. Pour beans into crock. Combine sugar, salt, pepper and dry mustard and put over top of beans. Pour on molasses. Add enough water to cover top of beans; drop in remaining bacon chunks and cover.

Bake in 325° oven for 5 or 6 hours until beans taste tender and are browned. Keep the beans covered with liquid during baking, adding hot water if necessary. When they are just about ready, uncover and let bake 30 minutes to let the liquid condense and help to brown beans.

Note: If salt pork is used, reduce salt to ½ teaspoon.

Jeannette Werner
Santa Fe, Texas

TEXAS BEANS

1 15-ounce can pork and beans
1 15-ounce can kidney beans
1 15-ounce can lima beans
1 large onion, chopped
1 clove garlic, chopped
1 tablespoon cumin seed
1 tablespoon Worcestershire sauce
1 tablespoon instant coffee granules
Pinch of oregano
Pinch of basil
Dash Tabasco
¼ cup brown sugar
½ cup ketchup
6 slices bacon

Combine all ingredients except bacon slices in 2- or 3-quart casserole. Top with bacon slices and bake covered at 350° for 1 hour. Uncover and bake another 30 minutes.

Janet Kiersted
Houston, Texas

COWPOKE BEANS

2 pounds pinto beans, soaked overnight and drained
1 teaspoon red pepper
2 teaspoons salt
2 cloves garlic, minced
8 slices bacon, chopped
3 cups onions, chopped and sautéed
2 1-pound cans stewed tomatoes
1 teaspoon ground cumin
1 teaspoon marjoram
10 teaspoons chili powder
Salt to taste

Cover beans with water and add red pepper, salt, garlic and bacon. Cook covered until tender, about 1½ hours. Meanwhile, simmer the sautéed onion, canned tomatoes, cumin, marjoram, chili powder and salt for 45 minutes. Add to the cooked beans and allow to simmer another 20 minutes.

Helen Hopmann
East Bernard, Texas

SALLIE'S BEST BEANS

2 cups dried pinto beans, thoroughly washed and picked
6 cups water
3 to 4 cloves garlic, sliced
¼ cup bacon drippings or 2 slices bacon
Salt to taste
Chopped cilantro (optional)

Soak beans overnight. In a large pot, cook beans in the water they soaked in and add enough water to make approximately 6 cups. (For the tastiest beans, do not add any water during the cooking process.) Bring to a boil, and when the beans float to the top, add garlic. Cover, and reduce heat to simmer. Cook beans covered for 2 to 3 hours, stirring occasionally.

Add drippings or bacon and cook covered for 45 minutes more or until broth becomes a light brown. Test beans for tenderness. Add salt only at the end of the cooking to prevent tough beans. If beans seem too watery, simply leave the lid off the pot for the final cooking time to reduce the liquid. Just before serving, stir in the cilantro.

Anne Thorpe
Houston, Texas

SMOKED BEANS

1 or 2 pounds pinto beans
1-2 tablespoons baking soda
2 cups smoked-meat broth
3 or 4 cups water
1 tablespoon cumin
3 cloves garlic
2 tablespoons garlic salt or powder
2 tablespoons chili powder
1 small onion, chopped
1 8-ounce can tomato sauce
3 or 4 teaspoons tortilla flour
Picante sauce (optional)

Soak pinto beans overnight with baking soda. The next day rinse the beans and put them in a 5-quart stew pot. Add the broth, water, cumin, garlic, garlic salt, chili powder and onion. Cook the beans until they are tender, then add the can of tomato sauce and stir well. When beans have cooked some more, add the tortilla flour to the pot to thicken the juice.

Eileen King
Lampasas, Texas

PINTO BEANS, PUERTO RICO STYLE

4 strips bacon, chopped
1 clove garlic, mashed
Pinch cumin
4 olives
1 tomato, chopped

Fry bacon. Mix remaining ingredients and pour into hot grease; simmer. Pour mixture into cooked beans.

Crispina Babbitt
Austin, Texas

MEXICAN BLACK-EYED PEAS

1 pound dried black-eyed peas (soaked in water 4—8 hours)
Ham bone or ham scraps
2 onions, chopped
1 No. 2 can tomatoes, undrained
3 cups celery, chopped
1 teaspoon chili powder
1 teaspoon salt (optional)
Freshly ground black pepper

Drain soaked peas. Add ham, onions and fresh water to cover, and cook slowly for several hours until peas are tender. Then add tomatoes, celery and seasoning to taste. Add fresh ground pepper and let simmer until thoroughly cooked.

Ernestine Gilmore
Conroe, Texas

BLACK-EYED PEA CASSEROLE

6 slices bacon, fried crisp
1 cup chopped celery
1 cup chopped green peppers
1 cup chopped onions
1 No. 303 can black-eyed peas
1 No. 303 can tomatoes

Fry bacon in skillet until crisp. Drain on paper towels. In grease from bacon, simmer celery, green peppers and onions until done. Add peas, tomatoes and chopped bacon. Season with salt and pepper. Simmer about 20 minutes. If you like things a little spicy, add 1 can Rotel tomatoes and green chilies instead of regular tomatoes, or use half and half.

Joy Keener
Sweeny, Texas

BLACK-EYED PEA JAMBALAYA

1 onion, chopped
2 cloves garlic
½ bell pepper, chopped
1 stalk celery, chopped
Oil for sautéing
2 cups rice
2½ cups chicken broth
1 can Rotel tomatoes and green chilies, diced
1 can black-eyed peas (or fresh shelled)
1 cup cubed ham
1 pound smoked sausage, cut up

Sauté vegetables in oil. Add rice and cook until rice begins to fry. Add broth, Rotel tomatoes, peas, ham and sausage. Let come to a boil, stir, lower heat, cover and don't peek for 30 minutes. A dash of Tabasco never hurts if added with broth.

Peggy J. Doolan
Houston, Texas

BROCCOLI CASSEROLE

*2 packages frozen chopped broccoli, cooked as directed on
    package*
1 can mushroom soup
1 tablespoon chopped onion
1 cup grated cheese
1 cup mayonnaise
1 whole egg
1 package Pepperidge Farm Stuffing Mix
Butter

Mix well the first 6 ingredients, and put into a greased baking dish. Cover with dry Pepperidge Farm bread crumbs, dot with butter, and bake at 350° for 30 minutes.

Mary Anderson
Richmond, Texas

CONNIE'S SWEET-AND-SOUR CABBAGE

1 medium head green cabbage
1 small head purple cabbage
1 large yellow onion
¼ cup vegetable oil
3 medium-size Granny Smith apples
½ cup cider vinegar
½ cup brown sugar

Core and shred cabbages. In a large heavy pot, sauté onion until tender. Add cabbage and a little water, and bring to simmer. Core and quarter apples (do not peel), cut into small pieces, and add to cabbage. Mix vinegar and sugar together; add to cabbage and apples. Simmer until cabbage and apples are tender. Serves 8.

Connie Schultz
Galveston, Texas

CREAMED CABBAGE WITH DILL

4 cups shredded cabbage
¼ cup minced onion
2 tablespoons butter
3 ounces cream cheese, softened and cut in bits
*2 tablespoons fresh snipped dill (or 1 teaspoon dried dill
    weed)*
Salt and pepper to taste

In a large saucepan blanch cabbage in boiling salted water to cover for 3 minutes. Drain the cabbage well. In a saucepan sauté onion in butter until it is softened. Add the cabbage and toss mixture well. Add cream-cheese bits and cook the mixture over low heat, stirring until cheese is melted. Add dill, salt and pepper, and simmer the cabbage for 2 minutes more. Serves 3 or 4 people.

Bette Shoebotham
Spring, Texas

GERMAN RED CABBAGE

1 head (about 2 pounds) firm, fresh red cabbage
3 tablespoons bacon drippings
1 large onion, chopped
1½ teaspoons salt
¼ teaspoon pepper
¼ cup dry white wine
¼ cup cider vinegar
¼ cup sugar
1 apple, peeled and chopped (or ⅓ cup applesauce)

Wash and shred cabbage. Place bacon drippings in a large pot with a tight lid, heat, add onions and sauté a little, but don't brown. Add the cabbage, stirring well to coat all the cabbage with the onion mixture. Cover and let steam over low heat about 15 minutes. Add the rest of the ingredients, stir well, cover and let steam over very low heat for about 30 minutes. Test for tenderness and seasonings. If it's too sweet, add a little vinegar, or add a little sugar if you like it sweeter. Serve it tender-crisp, not soggy.

Jeannette Werner
Santa Fe, Texas

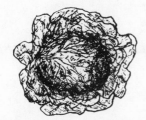

BAKED CAULIFLOWER

1 head cauliflower
2 tablespoons butter
2 tablespoons flour
1 cup milk
½ teaspoon salt
¼ teaspoon pepper
2 tablespoons chopped pimiento
½ cup chopped green onions
¼ cup buttered bread crumbs
1 tablespoon grated cheese

Cook cauliflower in about ¾ cup salted water for 20 minutes. Drain and place in baking dish. Melt butter in small skillet. Add flour and stir until blended. Gradually add milk, stirring until smooth and thick. Add salt, pepper, pimiento and green onions. Blend. Pour over cauliflower. Sprinkle with bread crumbs and grated cheese. Bake at 375° for 20 minutes or until lightly brown. Serves 4–6.

Bernice Murphy
Hobbs, New Mexico

MARINATED CARROTS

2 pounds carrots, cooked and diced
½ cup sugar
½ cup oil
¾ cup vinegar
1 bell pepper
1 can tomato soup
1 teaspoon prepared mustard
1 teaspoon Worcestershire sauce
Salt and pepper
1 onion, chopped fine

Wash and peel carrots, slice and cut in medium-size pieces. Cook and drain well, then cool. Mix the other ingredients and add carrots. Keep in refrigerator until ready to serve.

Mary Anderson
Richmond, Texas

GOLDEN CARROTS

2 cups carrots
3 tablespoons butter or margarine
¼ teaspoon salt
3 or 4 tablespoons water
¼ teaspoon ginger
¼ cup parsley sprigs

Peel and finely dice or slice carrots. Melt butter or margarine in saucepan. Add carrots, salt, water and ginger, and mix well. Cover and cook (steam) over medium heat for 20 minutes, until tender. Garnish with parsley. Yields 3 to 4 servings.

Ruth Ray
Houston, Texas

EXOTIC CELERY

6 ribs celery, sliced in ½-inch pieces
½ cup onion, thinly sliced
Butter
1 8-ounce can sliced water chestnuts, drained
½ cup slivered almonds
1 10¾-ounce can cream of mushroom soup
½ cup cheddar cheese, grated

Sauté celery and onion in small amount of butter till crisp-tender. Add water chestnuts, almonds and soup. Stir well. Pour into 1-quart casserole dish. Sprinkle cheese on top. Bake at 350° for 20 minutes or until bubbly. Serves 6.

Mary Easley
Rosenberg, Texas

CORN CASSEROLE, CREOLE STYLE

1 onion, chopped fine
3 tablespoons chopped sweet green pepper
5 tablespoons vegetable oil
1 No. 2 can yellow cream-style corn
1 egg, beaten
2 cups milk
½ cup yellow cornmeal
Red pepper, salt and black pepper to taste
Bread crumbs
Butter

Wilt onions and green pepper in hot oil. Add corn and cook about 15 minutes. Mix beaten egg and milk. Pour slowly into above mixture. Add cornmeal slowly. Season to taste with peppers and salt. Cook until the consistency of mush. Pour into buttered casserole dish. Spread bread crumbs over this; dot with butter. Bake at 375° for 45 minutes. Serves 6.

Rosalie Jordan
Houston, Texas

CORN WITH ZIP

3 cans Mexican-style corn, drained
4 ounces cream cheese with chives
2 tablespoons picante sauce

Mix all ingredients and cook over low heat.

Donna R. Grabs
Austin, Texas

"Fast and easy and so good."

GULLIVER'S CREAMED CORN

20 ounces frozen whole-kernel corn
8 ounces whipping cream
8 ounces milk
1 teaspoon salt
6 teaspoons sugar
Pinch cayenne pepper
2 tablespoons butter, melted
2 tablespoons flour

Combine all ingredients except butter and flour in a pot, and bring to a boil. Simmer 5 minutes. Blend butter with flour; add to corn mixture, stirring until well blended and mixture thickens. Remove from heat.

Variation: Put finished corn in heat-proof casserole, sprinkle with Parmesan cheese, and place under broiler until brown. Serves 8.

Gayle Yoder
Seabrook, Texas

RICHMOND PLAZA BAPTIST CHURCH BAKED CORN

6 tablespoons margarine
¼ cup yellow cornmeal
1 can whole-kernel corn
1 can cream-style corn
1 small can chopped green chilies (mild)
2 eggs, beaten
½ teaspoon garlic salt
2 cups grated sharp cheese

Melt margarine in a 1½-quart baking dish. Mix remaining ingredients in a bowl and pour into the baking dish. Bake 1 hour at 350°.

Betty Woodring Wilson
Houston, Texas

"This baked corn recipe has been to more weddings, wakes, showers and Sunday School parties than any preacher I know."

MAQUE CHOUX

12 ears of corn
2 tablespoons butter, melted
1 medium onion, chopped
2 tablespoons tomatoes
2 tablespoons green chilies
½ green pepper, chopped
¼ to ½ teaspoon sugar
Salt and pepper

Run a sharp knife through each row of corn kernels. Cut corn from cob. Scrape cob to remove remaining pulp and juice. Combine all other ingredients with cut corn in heavy saucepan. Cook over low heat until corn is tender, stirring frequently.

Roy D. Plaisance
Angleton, Texas

MEXICAN CORN ZUCCHINI

1 pound small zucchini, thinly sliced
2½ to 3 cups canned corn, drained
¾ cup finely chopped onion
⅓ cup chopped green pepper
2 tablespoons oil
¼ teaspoon sugar
1 teaspoon salt
¼ teaspoon pepper
3 medium tomatoes, peeled and coarsely chopped
1½ cups bread cubes
⅓ cup diced sharp cheese

Mix all ingredients except tomatoes, bread and cheese. Cook over medium heat 10 to 12 minutes or until zucchini is done. Add tomatoes, and pour into baking dish. Sprinkle with bread and cheese. Bake until cheese melts and bread is crisp. Serves 6.

Betty Lou Warren
Texas City, Texas

CORN PUDDING

2 No. 2 cans corn (1 whole-kernel, 1 cream-style)
2 cups grated cheddar cheese
1 cup cornmeal
⅔ cup oil
1 4-ounce can chopped green chilies
1 teaspoon salt
½ teaspoon garlic powder
¼ teaspoon cayenne
4 well-beaten eggs
½ cup chopped onions

Mix first 8 ingredients well, then add eggs and onions. Pour into greased 2- to 3-quart casserole dish (shallow dish works best). Bake at 350° for 35 to 40 minutes.

Barbara Scherer
Columbus, Texas

EGGPLANT BAKE

1 large eggplant
1 medium onion, very finely diced
1 egg
Garlic powder
Pepper
1 package saltine crackers
1½ cups cheddar cheese, shredded

"I was born in Texas and have my roots as deep here as the bluebonnets. . . ."

Peel and cube eggplant. Cover with water and cook about 20 minutes or until tender. When tender, use a potato masher and mash eggplant completely. Don't drain liquid from eggplant. Add onion, egg (slightly beaten), a pinch of garlic powder and enough black pepper to taste. Mix this all together well and then add a whole package of crushed crackers. These are salty, so you don't need to add any other salt. Stir all together and pour into oiled casserole dish. Put the cheese on top and bake at 350° for 30 minutes.

Sandra Hollis
Huntsville, Texas

EGGPLANT PATTIES

1 medium eggplant
1¼ cups cracker crumbs
1¼ cups cheddar cheese, shredded
2 eggs, beaten
2 tablespoons chopped parsley
2 tablespoons chopped green onions
½ teaspoon salt
1 clove garlic, minced fine
⅛ teaspoon black pepper

Pare and cube eggplant and cook in water 5 minutes. Drain and mash. Add to the other ingredients. Mix well and shape into 8 patties. Fry in hot oil until golden brown on each side.

Ruth Talafuse
Wharton, Texas

FRESH GREENS

1 large bunch turnip, mustard or collard greens (about 2 to 2½ pounds)
¼ pound salt pork

Check leaves of fresh greens carefully. Remove pulpy stems and discolored spots on leaves. Wash thoroughly in several changes of water. Place greens in colander to drain.

Cook diced salt pork about 10 minutes in boiling water in covered pot. Add washed greens, a few at a time. Cover pot and cook slowly until greens are tender. Do not overcook. Add salt if needed.

An alternate method is to wash greens carefully and place in a large cooking pot with only the water that clings to the leaves.

Chopped turnip roots may be added to turnip greens when almost done. Add salt and bacon drippings after greens have cooked tender.

Mustard greens are good if cooked partially done in the water that clings to the leaves, then finished in bacon drippings. Serve with vinegar or pepper sauce.

Southern "pot-likker" is the liquid in which greens have been cooked. Those who like to have a quantity of liquid will need to add boiling water as the greens are cooking. A favorite way of serving "pot-likker" is over cornbread squares.

Miriam Nicholson
Houston, Texas

JALAPEÑO CHEESE GRITS

4½ cups water
1 teaspoon salt
1½ cups quick-cooking grits
4 cups (1 pound) sharp cheddar cheese, shredded
¼ cup butter
2 canned jalapeño peppers, seeded and chopped
2 tablespoons chopped pimiento
1 teaspoon salt
3 eggs, beaten

Combine water and 1 teaspoon salt in a large saucepan; bring to a boil. Gradually stir grits into water; cover, reduce heat to low, and cook 5 minutes, stirring occasionally. Add cheese and butter; stir until melted. Stir in peppers, pimiento, and 1 teaspoon salt. Add a small amount of hot grits to eggs, stirring well; stir egg mixture into the remaining grits. Pour grits into a lightly greased 12×8×2-inch baking dish. Bake, uncovered, at 350° for 30 minutes. Serves 8–10.

Dorothy Burgess
Huntsville, Texas

CREAMED PEAS AND EGGS

1 can English peas
3 tablespoons butter or margarine
3 tablespoons flour
½ teaspoon salt
¼ teaspoon pepper
⅔ cup milk
½ teaspoon sugar
4 hard-boiled eggs, quartered

Drain peas, saving liquid. Melt butter; blend in flour, salt and pepper. Add liquid from peas, stirring until well mixed. Add milk and heat to boiling point, stirring until slightly thickened. Add peas, sugar and eggs. When thoroughly heated, serve at once.

Charlotte Sheedy
Big Spring, Texas

SWEET POTATO SOUFFLE

2 cups sweet potatoes, mashed
¾ teaspoon salt
½ cup honey
3 eggs, beaten
1 to 1½ cups milk
2 tablespoons cornstarch
¾ cup pecans, chopped

Blend all ingredients. Pour into greased 1½-quart casserole dish and bake at 300° for 30 to 40 minutes or until done.

Ruth Branch
League City, Texas

SWEET POTATO PONE

2½ cups grated sweet potatoes
1 cup sugar
2 eggs, well beaten
1 tablespoon grated orange rind
1 teaspoon nutmeg
2 tablespoons melted butter
1 cup chopped nuts
¼ teaspoon cinnamon
¾ cup milk

Mix all ingredients and place in a greased casserole. Dot with additional butter. Bake at 350° for 45 minutes or until golden brown. Serves 6.

Bernice Box
Friendswood, Texas

POTATO DUMPLINGS

9 medium potatoes
1 teaspoon salt
3 eggs, well beaten
1 cup sifted flour
⅔ cup bread crumbs or Farina
Grated nutmeg

Boil potatoes with skins on until soft. Remove skins and press potatoes through ricer. Add salt, eggs, flour, ⅔ cup bread crumbs and nutmeg. Mix thoroughly. Form mixture into dry balls about the size of walnuts (if mixture is too moist, add more bread crumbs). Drop balls into boiling salted water. When balls come to surface, boil uncovered for 3 minutes. Remove one from liquid and cut open. If center is dry, they are sufficiently cooked. Remove balls from liquid and serve with mushroom or onion sauce. Serves 12.

MUSHROOM SAUCE:
4 tablespoons oil
4 tablespoons flour
2 cups stock from dumplings liquid
Salt and pepper
1 cup mushrooms

Make a brown sauce of oil, flour and stock. Season, add mushrooms and cook for 4 minutes for canned mushrooms or 6 minutes for fresh mushrooms.

ONION SAUCE:
¼ cup minced onion
3 tablespoons oil
3 tablespoons flour
1½ cups potato dumpling stock
1 teaspoon minced parsley

Cook onion with the oil until slightly browned. Stir in the flour. Then add the stock and parsley, stirring constantly until thick.

Betty J. Tanner
Port Lavaca, Texas

POTATO CASSEROLE WITH CHEESE

1½ cups milk
1 onion, peeled and sliced
1 bay leaf
¼ teaspoon thyme
Salt and pepper to taste
1 clove garlic
1 teaspoon butter
6 medium-size boiling potatoes
½ cup grated Swiss cheese
1 tablespoon butter

Preheat oven to 350°. In a saucepan, bring milk to simmering point with onion slices, bay leaf, thyme, salt, pepper and garlic. Remove from heat. Butter a casserole. Peel potatoes and cut into thin slices. Place a layer of potatoes in the casserole; add a third of the cheese. Layer potatoes and cheese until all have been used, finishing with a layer of potatoes. Strain milk over potatoes. Dot with butter. Cover and bake 45 minutes or until potatoes are tender. Serves 6.

Bette Shoebotham
Spring, Texas

STABLES POTATOES AU GRATIN

6 medium potatoes, boiled and diced
1 pint half-and-half
1 cup milk
3 tablespoons flour
3 tablespoons butter
Salt and pepper
½ pint sour cream
Bread crumbs
Paprika
1 cup shredded cheese
2 tablespoons dry white wine

Prepare the potatoes, then make a sauce of the half-and-half, milk, flour, butter, salt and pepper. Let cool, then add sour cream.

Mix sauce and potatoes (if too thick add more milk). Cover with bread crumbs and sprinkle with paprika. Put in a 2-quart casserole dish and bake at 350° until bubbly and potatoes are tender.

Remove from oven and sprinkle with wine and cheese. Return to oven for a few minutes to melt the cheese.

Petty Schoelman
Houston, Texas

SOME KIND OF POTATOES

8 potatoes, unpeeled
1 bay leaf
1½ cups sour cream
¼ cup butter, melted
1 can cream of chicken soup, undiluted
1 small onion, chopped
Salt and pepper
1½ cups grated cheese
1½ cups crushed potato chips

Boil potatoes in salted water with bay leaf. Cool, peel, and coarsely grate potatoes. Spread in an 8×13-inch buttered baking dish. Mix sour cream, melted butter, chicken soup, chopped onion, salt and pepper, and pour over potatoes. Bake 30 to 35 minutes at 350°. Remove from oven and sprinkle with grated cheese and potato chips. Bake 10 minutes more.

Sherwood W. Lamkin
Nacogdoches, Texas

SOUR CREAM POTATOES

3 cups new potatoes, cut in wedges
¼ cup butter
½ teaspoon salt
¼ teaspoon pepper
½ to 1 cup sour cream
½ cup grated cheddar cheese
¼ cup chopped green onions

Place potatoes in shallow buttered casserole, dot with butter, and sprinkle with salt and pepper. Cover casserole and bake at 375° for 30 to 40 minutes. Remove potatoes from oven, stir in sour cream and cheese, and return to oven. Bake 10 more minutes. Remove from oven, sprinkle with chopped green onions. Serves 6.

Bobbie Dykes
Bay City, Texas

HASHBROWN CASSEROLE

1 cup margarine
2 pounds frozen hashbrowns, thawed
2 cups cheddar cheese, shredded
½ cup chopped green onion
8 ounces sour cream
1 can cream of chicken soup
Salt and pepper
2 cups crumbled corn flakes

Melt half of margarine in a large glass baking dish. Mix the other ingredients (except margarine and corn flakes) in a large bowl. Bake 30 minutes at 350°. Mix corn flakes and remaining margarine. Sprinkle over casserole and bake for 15 minutes at 350°.

Beverly J. Harrison
Houston, Texas

OKRA PILAF

4 slices bacon, chopped
1 medium onion, chopped
½ medium green pepper, chopped
⅓ cup uncooked rice
2 cups sliced okra
1 1-pound can stewed tomatoes
Salt and pepper to taste

In large dutch oven, fry bacon until crisp; remove from pan and set aside. Add onion and green pepper to drippings and cook over medium heat, stirring often, until tender, about 5 minutes. Add rice, okra and tomatoes. Cook, stirring often, until liquid is absorbed and rice is tender, about 25 minutes. Stir in reserved bacon, and season to taste. Serves 4. If liquid is absorbed and rice is not tender, add a little water. Also, boiled shrimp can be added to mixture.

Annie Socha
El Campo, Texas

TEXAS-FRIED OKRA

2 cups okra, cut into pieces
1 egg, beaten with a tablespoon of water
½ cup cornmeal
¾ cup flour
½ teaspoon salt
¼ teaspoon pepper
Oil or shortening

Wash okra, cut off stems, and cut into bite-size pieces. Put in plastic, sealable container with egg and water. Shake to get egg mixture on all pieces of okra. In another large, sealable container, mix the cornmeal, about half the flour, and the salt and pepper. Using a slotted spatula, put about half the okra in the cornmeal mixture, cover and shake. Add more drained okra (and flour) to container as needed. Seal and shake until all okra is coated.

Dry the slotted spatula and use to put okra in pan with hot oil. Fry until golden and crisp. Use a 10-inch skillet with enough oil for okra to float. Prepare and fry about 1 cup at a time, using medium-high temperature. Drain okra on paper towels. Salt to taste.

Shirley Knight
Georgetown, Texas

CRISPY ONION RINGS

2 sweet Spanish onions
1 cup pancake mix
¾ cup beer
Oil for deep frying (heated to 375°)
Salt

Peel onions and cut into ½-inch-thick slices; separate into rings. Combine pancake mix and beer to make a smooth batter. Dip onion rings in batter and fry a few at a time in hot oil until golden brown. Drain on absorbent-paper-lined baking sheet. Keep fried onion rings hot in oven until all rings are fried.

Stephanie Tillery
Lexington, Texas

PRICKLY PEAR

During the Great Depression in 1930–35, I lived with my husband and two small children on the once-famous Gray Ranch (La Gloria) in southwest Texas. Although my husband was ranch foreman, the income was very small.

I was pleased when the wives of the Mexican cowboys taught me to cook and serve the wild prickly pear that grew in abundance.

The leaves were gathered when they were so young that there were no spines. First they were washed, parboiled and drained.

Sometimes—

we added raw eggs and scrambled them in butter with salt and black pepper seasoning.

Sometimes—

we added canned tomatoes, onions, wild peppers and chili powder and served with roast beef or venison.

Sometimes—

we added eggs and flour and made patties and fried them in hot shortening.

Sometimes—

we did not boil but sliced them very thin, dipped them in egg and milk batter, rolled them in meal or flour and fried them to a golden brown. They were eaten like our potato chips.

I don't know the nutritional value, but do know it added to our "hum-drum" menus, filled our stomachs and quenched our appetites.

I am now 82 years old; however, I remember when I ate wild prickly pears.

Pearl Monaghan
The Woodlands, Texas

GREEN RICE

2 cups raw rice
1½ cups milk
½ cup salad oil
½ pound Velveeta, grated
½ pound cheddar cheese, grated
1 cup chopped parsley
1 cup chopped green pepper
1 cup chopped green onion
2 cloves garlic, chopped
Salt and pepper

Cook rice according to package directions. Stir remaining ingredients together in a large bowl. Stir warm rice into other ingredients until cheeses are melted. Pour into a large casserole or baking dish. Bake at 350° for 1 hour. Serves 12.

Margaret Nelson
Baytown, Texas

RICE CHILE VERDE

3 cups sour cream
5 cups cooked rice
1 cup green mild chilies, chopped (use canned)
1 pound Monterey jack jalapeño cheese
Green onion tops, chopped
Cheddar cheese, grated

Mix first 5 ingredients and place in a greased casserole.

Top with cheddar cheese. Bake at 350° for about 30 minutes or until cheese is melted. This can be made ahead and refrigerated or frozen until ready to use.

Gayle Yoder
Seabrook, Texas

DRESSING AS A SIDE DISH

6 ounces mixed long-grain and wild rice
1½ cups chopped celery
1½ cups sliced mushrooms
½ cup butter
1 8-ounce package herb-seasoned stuffing mix
1 cup hot water
1 2-ounce jar sliced pimientos
½ cup chopped parsley

Cook rice as directed. Sauté celery and mushrooms in butter. Add stuffing mix and hot water. Add to cooked rice along with celery and mushrooms. Stir in drained pimientos and parsley. Bake 20 to 30 minutes at 350°.

Mrs. J. P. Pfieffer
Bastrop, Texas

SPINACH MADELEINE

2 packages frozen chopped spinach
4 tablespoons butter
1 small onion
2 tablespoons flour
¾ teaspoon garlic powder
6 ounces jalapeño cheese
½ cup milk
¾ teaspoon celery salt
1 tablespoon Worcestershire sauce
Buttered bread crumbs

Cook spinach. Drain and save ½ cup juice. Melt butter and sauté onion; add flour, spinach juice, garlic powder, cheese, milk, celery salt and Worcestershire sauce. Mix well. Pour into a 1½-quart baking dish. Cover with buttered crumbs and bake at 350° until bubbly.

Jean Winters
Burton, Texas

SPINACH SERGIU

1 pound fresh spinach
Creole seasoning blend
6 to 8 slices fried bacon, crumbled
3 tablespoons horseradish
Tabasco
Dry white wine
Worcestershire sauce

Cook the spinach in a small amount of water seasoned with a Creole-style dry seasoning blend; drain. Mix with crumbled fried bacon and horseradish and a few dashes of Tabasco, white wine and Worcestershire sauce. Warm mixture on low to medium heat for about 5 minutes.

S. Vance Percy
Seabrook, Texas

STUFFED SQUASH

5 medium yellow squash
¾ cup chopped onion
½ cup chopped celery
1 pound lean ground meat
½ pound Owens hot sausage
½ cup Italian bread crumbs
4 tablespoons Parmesan cheese
1 8-ounce can tomato sauce
½ teaspoon salt
½ teaspoon pepper
1 4-ounce can mushrooms, chopped and drained
Parmesan cheese for topping

Parboil whole squash in slightly salted water until easily pierced with fork. Drain and core. Split squash lengthwise and gently edge around center of squash and spoon out the pulp of squash. Set pulp aside. In a large skillet, sauté onions and celery until transparent. Set aside. Brown both meats together. Drain well.

In a large dutch oven, place meats, onion, celery, squash pulp, bread crumbs, 4 tablespoons Parmesan cheese, tomato sauce, salt, pepper and mushrooms. Mix well and cook 10 minutes. Spoon meat mixture into squash shells. In a long casserole dish, place stuffed squash, putting the grated Parmesan cheese on the top. Bake at 375° for 40 minutes.

Donna R. Grabs
Austin, Texas

SQUASH CASEROLE

1 egg, lightly beaten
½ onion, chopped
1 10-ounce can cream of mushroom soup
¼ cup margarine, softened
½ cup crushed Ritz crackers
2 cups cooked squash, drained
Dash pepper

Combine all ingredients. Place in a greased casserole dish and bake at 350° for 30 minutes or until hot and bubbly. Serves 6.

Mamie Anthony
Nacogdoches, Texas

SQUASH DRESSING

2 cups cooked squash
½ stick margarine
1 large onion, chopped
½ cup chopped celery
½ cup chopped green pepper
1 cup chopped mushrooms
2 cups crumbled cornbread
1 can cream of mushroom soup
Salt and pepper

Combine all ingredients in casserole. Bake 30 to 40 minutes at 350°.

Cindy Stubblefield
Stafford, Texas

STUFFED TOMATOES

4 medium tomatoes
4 teaspoons olive oil
2 tablespoons fresh minced parsley
1 tablespoon fresh minced basil
½ teaspoon dried oregano
1 clove garlic, crushed
½ teaspoon salt
Pepper to taste
¼ cup Parmesan cheese mixed with ¼ cup bread crumbs
¼ cup bread crumbs mixed with 2 tablespoons melted butter

Slice off tops of tomatoes and scoop out inside, leaving ¼-inch shell of tomato. Chop the pulp coarsely and put in bowl with olive oil, parsley, basil, oregano, garlic, salt, pepper and Parmesan cheese. Spoon the filling into the tomato shells. Top with buttered bread crumbs and bake in 350° oven in a shallow baking pan for 20 minutes. Makes 4 servings.

Connie Henderson
Austin, Texas

RELISHES
AND
PRESERVES

JALAPEÑO JELLY

1 red bell pepper
1 green bell pepper
2 jalapeño peppers, red if possible (a few more if you are
    brave or really like hot stuff)
1½ cups white vinegar
6½ cups sugar
1 bottle fruit pectin

Chop all peppers very fine or process in blender. Combine peppers, vinegar and sugar in kettle; bring to a rolling boil. Set aside for 10 minutes. Stir in fruit pectin. Let sit for 10 minutes. Pour into sterilized jars and seal. Makes about five 8-ounce jars.

Gay Cantrell
Houston, Texas

"This is great on steaks, cornbread, green beans, peas or carrots, or pour over cream cheese, or mix with sour cream for a Texas-style dip. Use with sausages, roasts, lamb or grilled cheese, Chinese food or even peanut-butter sandwiches."

CHOWCHOW

1 gallon chopped cabbage
12 green peppers, chopped
2 quarts green tomatoes, chopped
½ cup salt
4 tablespoons mustard seeds
3 tablespoons celery seeds
2 tablespoons mixed whole pickling spice
4 tablespoons ground mustard
1 tablespoon ground ginger
1 tablespoon ground turmeric
12 onions, chopped
12 red peppers, chopped
5 cups sugar
2 to 3 quarts white vinegar

Mix cabbage, green peppers and tomatoes with salt, and let stand overnight. Drain. Tie mixed whole spices in a cheesecloth bag, and add to sugar and vinegar. Simmer for 20 minutes. Add all other ingredients and simmer until mixture is hot and well seasoned. Remove spice bag, pack in hot jars and seal at once.

Bernice Box
Friendswood, Texas

HOT PEPPER RELISH

½ gallon jalapeño peppers
5 onions
2 cups sugar
1 teaspoon salt
1 quart vinegar

Grind peppers and onions. Mix together with other ingredients. Bring to a boil and cook for 30 minutes, until pepper has lost its green color. Place in sterilized jars. Yields 4 or 5 pints.

Note: You should grind the peppers and cook in a well-ventilated place. You may include some red-colored pepper, to add some color to the relish. You may also alter the amount of sugar according to personal taste.

Kenneth D. Baker
Lufkin, Texas

DOT'S PEPPER JELLY APPETIZER

4 large bell peppers, seeded
12 jalapeño peppers, seeded
1½ cups cider vinegar
6½ cups sugar
1 6-ounce bottle fruit pectin
Green food coloring
Cream cheese
Crackers

Chop peppers in blender. In saucepan, bring peppers, vinegar and sugar to a boil and boil 10 minutes. Strain if desired. Add fruit pectin; boil 1 minute. Add food coloring to desired color. Pour into 6 sterilized jars. Serve jelly over a block of cream cheese, with crackers, as an appetizer.

Dorothy Ann Rothermel
Brenham, Texas

PICANTE SAUCE

2 large cloves garlic, minced
1 tablespoon mustard seed
1 large onion, chopped
1 large bell pepper, chopped
2 large jalapeño peppers, chopped (remove seeds)
3 quarts fresh tomatoes, peeled and diced
1 cup sugar
1 cup vinegar
5 teaspoons salt

Tie garlic and mustard seeds in cloth. Mix all ingredients and simmer uncovered until cooked down to a thick sauce, about 45 minutes to an hour. Pack in jars and seal. Process in hot-water bath 35 minutes. Makes about 6 pints.

Mrs. Hershel Orr
West Columbia, Texas

PEAR RELISH

Lemon juice
1 peck pears (2 gallons), peeled and cored
1 dozen medium white onions
1 dozen sweet bell peppers
1 dozen red hot peppers
3 teaspoons salt (optional)
3 cups sugar
2 cups prepared mustard
2 teaspoons celery seed
2 cups cider vinegar

Sprinkle lemon juice on pears. Prepare vegetables, then put fruit and vegetables through a food grinder. Add rest of ingredients and cook 30 minutes. Pour into jars and seal while hot.

Josephine Miller Bush
Huntsville, Texas

APRICOT-PEAR BUTTER OR RELISH

Enough fresh pears to make 5 cups pear pulp
1 6-ounce package dried apricots (soak 1 hour and grind
* with pears)*
Water
4 cups sugar
1 teaspoon cinnamon
1 teaspoon allspice

Peel, core and grind pears. Soak apricots in water for 1 hour; drain and grind. Mix pears and apricots, place in pot and add water to just cover fruits. Add remainder of ingredients and simmer uncovered until thick and bubbly, about 90 minutes. Pack in hot jars and seal.

Mrs. Hershel Orr
West Columbia, Texas

APPLE BUTTER

1 gallon applesauce
2 pounds dark brown sugar
1 tablespoon allspice
1 tablespoon cloves
1½ tablespoons cinnamon
Few drops red food coloring

Cook in slow electric cooker with lid on for 15 to 18 hours. Needs to be stirred about once an hour. Seal in clean jars.

Margie M. Cook
Livingston, Texas

RIPE TOMATO RELISH

12 large ripe tomatoes
6 medium onions, coarsely chopped
6 bell peppers, coarsely chopped
3 hot peppers, chopped
1½ cups cider vinegar
1½ cups sugar

Peel and cut tomatoes into eighths. Place in large pan and add onions, bell peppers and hot peppers. Cook until natural juices are reduced and mixture is thick. Add cider vinegar and sugar. Mix well. Bring to a boil and cook for 10 to 15 minutes. If mixture gets too thick, add ½ cup more cider vinegar.

Seal in hot sterilized jars and process 5 minutes in hot-water bath. Makes 6 pints.

Nita Rivoire
Sugar Land, Texas

COUNTRY TOMATO JAM

4½ pounds tomatoes, peeled
4½ cups sugar
1½ cups vinegar
1 tablespoon cinnamon
½ teaspoon allspice
1 teaspoon cloves

Scald, peel and quarter tomatoes. Put in pan to cook. Add sugar, vinegar and spices. Simmer slowly until thickened, then put in sterilized jars and seal.

Dortha Altman
Conroe, Texas

WATERMELON RIND PICKLES

Prepare rind by cutting off all green and pink. Cut into strips to make about a gallon of strips. Dissolve 2 tablespoons calcium hydroxide (obtained from a drugstore) in 1 gallon of water in a stoneware crock. Soak rinds overnight (it is a good idea to put this in the refrigerator). Sometimes it may take 2 or 3 days for the rinds to become crisp and clear through. Wash in clear water and put on to boil in clear water. Empty off the water and boil again in clear water. Drain.

SYRUP:
5 pounds sugar
1 quart cider vinegar
1 cup water
3 tablespoons whole cloves
3 tablespoons whole allspice
3 sticks cinnamon

Blend ingredients in a large pot and bring to a rolling boil. Add rinds and cook at a low boil until rinds are tender when pierced with a broomstraw. This may take up to 3 hours of slow cooking. Stir to keep rinds from sticking.

It may be necessary to add small amounts of water if the syrup becomes too thick, or add more sugar if the liquid does not have the consistency of table syrup.

When rinds are crisp, clear but tender, pack into sterilized jars, cover with syrup, seal and store in a cool, dark closet.

Ruby Baty
Wharton, Texas

CRYSTAL DILL PICKLES

Start 3 to 4 weeks before you want to serve the pickles. Drain the juice from a jar of your favorite dill pickles. Cut the pickles into spears lengthwise. Place carefully back into pickle jar (no juice) and cover with granulated sugar. Shake to make the sugar go down. Cover and place in refrigerator. The next day, turn jar upside down a few times, and add more sugar to cover pickles. This may be repeated several times until sugar is dissolved and pickles are covered in juice. Refrigerate and pickles will become very crisp and good.

Jeannette Werner
Santa Fe, Texas

WICKEL'S PICKLES

(Kosher Dill Pickles)

1 quart vinegar
3 quarts water
1 cup salt

Combine ingredients and bring to boil, then take off heat. Cool and store extra brine for future use.

For 1 pint of pickles:
Cucumbers—enough for 1 pint jar, washed with tops and bottoms pared
Fresh dill, 2 or 3 sprigs
½ teaspoon pickling spice
Dash dry mustard
1 slice bell pepper
1 slice onion
1 or more cloves garlic
¼ teaspoon alum
Dash turmeric

Pack all ingredients except brine into sterilized pint jar with some of the dill in the bottom of the jar and some on top of the cucumbers. Pour hot brine over contents of jar to within ½ inch of jar top. Adjust lid and seal, then immerse jars in boiling water bath approximately 5 minutes to assure seal. Store 6 weeks before using to allow proper ripening.

Jolene Wickel
La Porte, Texas

SWEET-HOT PICKLES

1 gallon jar whole sour pickles
5 pounds sugar
6 cloves garlic, chopped
1 small bottle Tabasco sauce

Drain and discard juice from pickles. Slice pickles about ½-inch thick. Blend sugar and chopped garlic. Refill gallon jar, alternating layers of sliced pickles and sugar/garlic mixture. Press pickles down in jar so they will all fit back into the gallon jar. Pour whole bottle of Tabasco sauce on top and seal. Let stand right side up for 1 day, upside down for 1 day, right side up 1 day, etc., for 6 days. After 6 days, pickles are ready. Chill.

Lou Wilson
Alvin, Texas

SWEET ICE PICKLES

7 pounds cucumbers, sliced 1¼-inches thick
1½ cups pickling lime
3 quarts vinegar
4 pounds sugar
2 teaspoons salt
½ box pickling spice (tie in bag)

Place cucumbers in water to cover and add lime; soak 24 hours. Drain and rinse well. Soak in clear water 2 hours.
Make a syrup of 4 remaining ingredients. Add drained cucumbers. Cook 2 hours or until cucumbers are clear in color. Pack cukes in jars and cover with hot syrup. Seal.

Yvonnie Roane
Houston, Texas

BREAD AND BUTTER PICKLES

12 medium cucumbers
6 small onions
1 teaspoon salt
1 cup vinegar
1½ cups sugar
1 teaspoon mustard seed
1 tablespoon black peppercorns (whole)

"This was my grand-mother's pickle recipe."

Slice cukes and onions and let stand 1 hour. Add the rest of ingredients. Boil 15 minutes. Put in hot sterilized jars and seal immediately.

Nita Rivoire
Sugar Land, Texas

SQUASH PICKLES

5 pounds yellow crookneck and zucchini squash
2 large bell peppers
2 large onions
4 ounces pimientos
¾ cup salt
3⅓ cups white vinegar
2 to 3 cups sugar (depending on your taste)
3 teaspoons celery seed
1½ teaspoons mustard seed
1½ teaspoons dill seed

Slice squash, peppers, onions and pimientos. Let stand 1 hour in salt. Rinse in cold water to remove all salt. Combine with remaining ingredients. Put all in a large pan and bring to a boil. Remove from burner. Cool a few minutes. Seal in sterilized jars while hot. Wait a month before eating—best when eaten cold.

Adelene C. Engelbrecht
Houston, Texas

GREEN TOMATO SWEET-AND-SOUR RELISH

4 cups diced onions
1 medium head cabbage
12 cups diced green tomatoes
6 red bell peppers
½ cup pickling salt
4 cups sugar
2 tablespoons mustard seed
1 tablespoon celery seed
1½ teaspoons turmeric
4 cups vinegar

"Especially tasty after it has aged a month or more."

Using a coarse blade, grind all vegetables in food grinder. (A blender can be used, using the chop button very lightly for a couple of seconds.) Sprinkle pickling salt over chopped vegetables in an enamel pan. Let vegetables stand overnight. The next day, rinse well and drain. Combine all other ingredients and pour over the vegetables. Mix well. Bring to a boil and cook for 10 minutes. Fill jars and seal. Process in hot-water bath for 5 minutes. Makes 9 pints.

Esther Krizan
Midland, Texas

BREADS

SIX-WEEK MUFFINS

1 15-ounce box raisin bran
3 cups sugar
5 cups flour
5 teaspoons baking soda
2 teaspoons salt
4 eggs, beaten
1 cup oil
1 quart buttermilk

Mix bran, sugar, flour, soda and salt in large bowl. Add eggs, oil and buttermilk and mix well. Store in covered container in refrigerator and bake as needed. Bake in greased hot muffin tins at 375° for 15 to 20 minutes.

Do not try to bake immediately after mixing. Makes better muffins if allowed to sit overnight in refrigerator. Batter should keep for 6 weeks.

Nita Rivoire
Sugar Land, Texas

BRAN MUFFINS

1 cup hot water
1 cup Nabisco 100% Bran
1 cup sugar
1¼ sticks margarine
2 eggs
2½ cups flour
2½ teaspoons soda
½ teaspoon salt
2 cups buttermilk
2 cups All-Bran

Pour hot water over bran. Cream butter, margarine and eggs. Sift flour, soda and salt together. Stir bran mixture into creamed mixture, then add remaining ingredients.

Spoon into lightly greased muffin tins and bake at 375° for 30 to 35 minutes. This mixture will keep for up to 6 weeks in a tightly closed container in your refrigerator.

Elizabeth Sadler
Houston, Texas

GOOD HEALTH MUFFINS

1 cup All-Bran with Extra Fiber cereal
1 cup whole wheat flour
1 egg
½ teaspoon artificial sweetener
2 tablespoons safflower oil
3 teaspoons baking powder
¼ teaspoon salt substitute
1 cup lowfat milk
1 cup raisins (optional)

Mix these ingredients thoroughly. Pour batter into muffin tins lightly greased with oil. Bake at 350° for 30 minutes. Makes 12 muffins.

Note: Sift flour for extra light muffins. May substitute unsalted pecans or walnuts for raisins. May use ½ cup raisins and ½ cup unsalted nuts.

Barbara A. Harper
Austin, Texas

MARY JEAN FERRELL'S AWARD-WINNING APRICOT ROLL

"Mary Jean Ferrell lives in Wallis, Texas, with her family and was the winner of the Czechfest baking contest for 1987. She stole the honor from her mother, Anny Nowak, who was last year's winner. When Mary Jean won the show, she won our hearts as well; she cried and so did the judges!"

2 packages dry yeast
1½ cups lukewarm water
2 cups flour
½ cup sugar
½ teaspoon salt
1 stick butter
2 eggs
2½ to 3½ cups flour

Dissolve yeast in water (about 10 minutes). Mix the first 7 ingredients, beating by hand or with a mixer on high for 2 minutes.

Slowly add flour as needed. (The amount here may vary, thus the 2½- to 3½-cup spread.) This should form a nice dough. Let it rest about 10 minutes, then knead with a spoon in the bowl.

Divide the dough equally and roll ½-inch thick. Spread first the cream-cheese mixture, then the fruit filling.

CREAM-CHEESE MIXTURE:
2 8-ounce packages cream cheese
2 cups sugar
1 teaspoon vanilla

Mix above ingredients and spread on rolled dough.

FRUIT FILLING:
You can use a prepared filling or dried apricots stewed

with sugar to taste. Spread on top of cream cheese mixture.

Now roll up like a jelly roll, tuck in the ends and brush with butter or simply grease the rolls. Let them rise until doubled in size and bake at 350° for 30 to 35 minutes. Ice when cooled.

Kathie Turner
KPRC Staff Member
Houston, Texas

APPLE STRUDEL

DOUGH:
½ cup warm milk
¾ stick margarine, melted
1 egg yolk
1½ cups flour

Mix all ingredients well and refrigerate at least 3 hours or overnight (best overnight).

FILLING:
6 cups tart apples, peeled and sliced
¾ cup raisins
½ cup flaked coconut
¾ cup sugar

Mix filling ingredients together.

2 cups soft bread crumbs (make in blender)
1 stick margarine, melted

Divide strudel dough into 2 parts. Roll out very thin on a tea towel. Brush each part with melted margarine and spread each with 1 cup soft bread crumbs. Divide apple mixture in half and place on one end of each piece of dough. Roll dough up with tea towel and place on large baking pan lined with double thickness of heavy foil. Brush strudel all over with melted margarine before baking. Bake 30 minutes at 325°.

Marie Zalesak
Houston, Texas

PECAN COFFEE CAKE

½ cup shortening
1 cup sugar
2 eggs and yolk of a third, well beaten
1½ cups flour
½ teaspoon salt
1 teaspoon baking powder
½ teaspoon vanilla
½ cup (or more) pecan halves

Cream shortening with sugar. Add the rest of the ingredients, except pecans, in order listed. This makes a very thick dough. Spread ¼-inch thick in an 8×12- or 9×13-inch pan. Sprinkle dough with fresh pecans, then cover with the following frosting:

"This is my Aunt Betty Stanley's Pecan Coffee Cake . . . straight from Carthage, Missouri. There's nothing like it."

1 egg white
1 cup brown sugar
½ teaspoon vanilla

Beat egg white (left-over from above yolk). Fold in brown sugar. (Always pack brown sugar into cup.) Add vanilla. Spread over dough and pecans. Bake about 25 minutes at 350°. Cut into squares before cake cools.

Bill Springer
Producer
The Eyes of Texas

SOUR CREAM COFFEE CAKE

½ pound butter or margarine
2 cups sugar
4 eggs
2 teaspoons vanilla
2 cups sour cream
3 cups flour
2 teaspoons soda

CRUMB MIXTURE:
1 cup sugar
4 teaspoons cinnamon
½ cup ground nuts

Cream first 4 ingredients. Fold in sour cream. Sift flour and soda. Fold into mixture. Pour half of mixture into 8½ × 13½-inch pan. Sprinkle half of crumb mixture on top. Pour remaining batter on top. Sprinkle rest of crumb mixture on top. Stir in small swirls. Bake for 55 minutes at 350°.

Melissa Parrott
Houston, Texas

STREUSEL-KUCHEN
(German Coffee Cake)

BASIC SWEET DOUGH:
2 cups scalded milk
2 packages yeast
¾ cup shortening
½ cup butter or margarine
½ cup sugar
2 teaspoons salt
4 egg yolks or 2 whole eggs, beaten
1 teaspoon cardamom
6 cups sifted flour
1 cup chopped pecans or 1 cup raisins (optional)
2 tablespoons milk

STREUSEL (TOPPING):
2 cups flour
2 cups sugar (1¼ cups white sugar and ¾ cup brown sugar, packed)
4 teaspoons ground cinnamon
¼ teaspoon ground nutmeg
2 teaspoons grated lemon rind
1 cup butter or margarine

Cool scalded milk to warm (110°) and sprinkle yeast over top. Let stand to soften. Cream shortening and butter; add sugar and salt. Cream together until light and fluffy. Add egg yolks (or whole eggs), and yeast, milk, cardamom, and enough flour to make a soft dough. Knead until smooth and elastic on lightly floured cloth or board. Place in greased bowl; cover and let rise until double in bulk (about 1 hour). Knead dough down (if desired, add pecans or raisins) and roll half of dough into 9 × 13-inch rectangle. Fit into 9 × 13-inch greased pan. Repeat with remaining dough. Make sure dough fills pan; press down firmly. Brush each cake with 1 tablespoon milk.

Make streusel topping: Combine flour, sugar, cinnamon, nutmeg, lemon rind and salt. Cut in butter or margarine until crumbly. Sprinkle half of topping over each cake. Let rise for 15 to 20 minutes. Bake at 350° for 30 to 40 minutes or until browned.

Amelia F. Mettke
Austin, Texas

SITTERLE'S COFFEE CAKE

1 yeast cake
¼ cup warm water
½ cup shortening
½ cup sugar
1 teaspoon salt
¼ teaspoon cinnamon
2 eggs
6½ to 7 cups flour, sifted
2 cups scalded milk, cooled
1 stick butter, melted

TOPPING:
2½ pints whipping cream
8 ounces sour cream
9 to 10 tablespoons sugar
Cinnamon
Additional flour
Additional butter

"This was baked each Saturday morning to be served for Sunday breakfast at the Chris Sitterle home in Victoria, Texas."

Dissolve yeast in warm water. Cream shortening, sugar, salt and cinnamon. Add eggs, beating well. Then add yeast. Add flour about 2 cups at a time alternately with milk. Beat well after each addition of flour. After all flour has been added, continue stirring dough until the back of your spoon doesn't stick to dough. Then put in large greased bowl or pot. Cover. Let rise about 2 hours in warm place. It should double in size. Divide into 6 pieces. Grease six 7 × 10¾-inch pans. Roll dough out, fit into pans and then let rise again about 45 minutes. (While they are rising, melt 1 stick of butter.)

For topping, mix whipping cream and sour cream together. After coffee cakes have risen the second time, brush tops with melted butter. Sprinkle about 2 tablespoons of sugar over the dough. Then add 4 tablespoons of cream mixture, then 2 of sugar, and sprinkle about 1 teaspoon flour over this. Add 2 more of sugar and dot with butter. Add 1 more tablespoon of cream and about 3 tablespoons of sugar, and shake cinnamon over the top. Bake at 375° for about 25 to 30 minutes. Makes 6 coffee cakes.

Jean King Sitterle
Houston, Texas

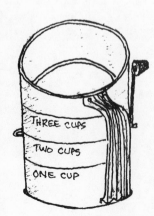

BUTTERMILK COFFEE CAKE
(Karnemelk Koffee Koek)

3 cups flour
2 cups sugar
¾ cup margarine
½ teaspoon cloves
1 teaspoon cinnamon
½ teaspoon nutmeg
2 teaspoons soda
2 cups buttermilk
Raisins as desired

Sift together the flour and sugar, and cut in the margarine until crumbly. Take out ½ cup and set aside. Add spices and soda to the flour mixture. Mix well; add buttermilk. Stir until all dry ingredients are moistened. Add raisins. Pour into a greased 9 × 13-inch pan. Sprinkle reserved mixture over top. Bake at 350° for 40 minutes.

Ruby Schafer
Houston, Texas

"An old Dutch recipe. . ."

KOLACHES

2 packages yeast
2½ cups warm milk
¼ cup sugar
3 cups flour

Combine and let sit for 30 minutes. Then add:
2 level teaspoons salt
½ cup shortening
½ cup sugar
3 eggs
4½ cups flour

Mix and let sit for 15 minutes, then work down. Let rise again until double in bulk. The dough should be soft and sticky. Three tablespoons of dough will make 1 roll. Bake about 25 to 30 minutes in a 375° oven.

Leona Zeller
Houston, Texas

HOT CAKES

2 whole eggs
1 cup milk
1 tablespoon vegetable oil
1 teaspoon sugar
2 teaspoons baking powder
Flour enough for thin batter

"This recipe came from a cafe at Millgate where my father, R. M. Brownlee, ate lunch once a week in 1914 when he went to collect rent from rent houses he owned near the gate of the cotton mill in McKinney, Texas. He liked the hot cakes so much they gave him the recipe."

Beat eggs with fork, add milk, oil, sugar, baking powder and flour in that order. Cook on griddle without fat.

Murray Cameron
Houston, Texas

WAFFLES I

2 eggs, separated
2 cups flour
3 tablespoons sugar
1 teaspoon salt
3 teaspoons baking powder
1¾ cups milk
4 tablespoons margarine, melted

Beat egg whites until stiff. Sift dry ingredients together. Add egg yolks and milk, beating until smooth. Add melted margarine and fold all into egg whites. Pour into waffle maker.

Yvonnie Roane
Houston, Texas

WAFFLES II

2 eggs, separated, whites beaten and set aside
1 teaspoon salt
1 tablespoon sugar
½ cup cooking oil
1 tablespoon vanilla
2 cups warm milk
2 packages yeast dissolved in ¼ cup warm water
3¼ cups flour

To egg yolks add salt, sugar, oil, vanilla, milk and yeast.

Gradually add the flour to liquid. Fold in beaten egg whites.

Oil waffle iron as directed and bake. Or the mixture can be refrigerated overnight. Add a little milk if batter is too thick. Can be served with fresh fruit, such as strawberries, and whipped cream.

Mrs. Jimmie Bush
The Woodlands, Texas

CORN FRITTERS

1 cup flour
1 teaspoon baking powder
1 teaspoon sugar
2 teaspoons salt
1 can cream-style corn
2 eggs, separated

Sift dry ingredients together and add to corn. Add egg yolks, well beaten, then fold in egg whites, beaten stiff. Drop by spoonfuls into hot vegetable oil and fry as griddle cakes.

Marianne Hayes
Markham, Texas

BUTTERMILK BISCUITS

2 cups flour
½ teaspoon salt
2 teaspoons baking powder
½ teaspoon baking soda
6 tablespoons shortening
¾ cup buttermilk

Sift dry ingredients together. Cut in shortening until mealy consistency is reached. Stir in buttermilk. Turn onto lightly floured board and knead lightly. Roll out to about ½-inch thickness and cut out with floured cutter. Bake in hot oven (475°) about 10 to 12 minutes.

Mrs. Salvador Brown
Dickinson, Texas

SIC 'EM, TIGERS, BREAKFAST SQUARES

2 cans refrigerated crescent-roll dough
1 pound bulk pork sausage
4 cups grated Monterey Jack and Swiss cheese
8 eggs
1⅔ cups milk
1 teaspoon salt
½ teaspoon pepper

Spray a 15 × 10 × 1-inch pan with cooking spray, and line it with crescent roll dough, to make a crust. Be sure your crust doesn't have any holes in it. Brown sausage until pink color is gone; drain and sprinkle on the crust. Add cheese to sausage layer. Whip eggs, milk, salt and pepper and pour on top. Bake in 425° oven about 20 minutes, until eggs are golden in color and a toothpick comes out clean.

Bacon, ham, onions and/or bell peppers can be added.

Helen Huber
Conroe, Texas

"I'm secretary for the Athletic Department at Conroe High School. The football coaches were always hungry on Friday mornings before the big game and wanted me to bring them food. It was hard to bring something that would feed a large group without a lot of trouble. So I created this all-in-one breakfast meal."

BUTTERMILK CORNBREAD

¼ cup flour
¼ teaspoon baking soda
½ teaspoon baking powder
½ teaspoon salt
1 cup cornmeal
1 egg
1 cup buttermilk
2 tablespoons salad oil

Sift flour, soda, baking powder and salt. Stir in cornmeal. Mix egg, milk and oil, and add to dry ingredients. Beat until smooth. Spoon into hot greased pan. Bake in hot oven (450°) for 20 to 25 minutes.

For muffins: Spoon into hot greased muffin pans, filling ⅔ full. Bake in hot oven (450°) for 10 to 15 minutes or until brown on top.

"Delicious with a pot of pinto beans."

E. Bushacker
Austin, Texas

CORNBREAD I

1 cup yellow cornmeal
1 cup all-purpose flour
4 teaspoons baking powder
½ teaspoon salt
1 cup milk
1 egg
¼ cup vegetable oil

Preheat oven to 425°. Mix all ingredients in order given. Place a little oil in pan and let it get warm in oven before putting mixture in. Bake in a hot oven for about 20 minutes.

Sarah Stewart
New Waverly, Texas

CORNBREAD II

¾ cup buttermilk or sour milk (or ¾ cup milk plus 2¼ teaspoons white vinegar)
1 egg
½ teaspoon baking soda
1 teaspoon baking powder
1 or 2 tablespoons sugar
1 teaspoon salt
4 tablespoons flour
1 cup cornmeal
3 tablespoons melted shortening

"This recipe comes from my grandmother, Mrs. Roy Davis Coles, who lives out in West Texas in Colorado City."

Beat milk and egg in a large mixing bowl. Combine dry ingredients; add to milk mixture. Add cornmeal, and then add shortening. Pour into a greased 8-inch-round pan. Bake in a 400° oven for 25 minutes.

Felice Ann Coles
Austin, Texas

CORNBREAD III

1 cup yellow cornmeal
1 cup white flour
4 teaspoons baking powder
1 teaspoon salt
1 egg, beaten
1 cup milk
¼ cup melted bacon drippings
¼ cup sugar
2 large jalapeños, seeds removed, chopped fine

Preheat oven to 350°. Grease a medium cast iron skillet or a 6 × 9-inch baking pan. Sift together first 4 ingredients, then beat in remaining ingredients. Pour into prepared pan and bake 35 to 40 minutes until golden brown.

Ann Reddehase
Houston, Texas

SURPRISE CORNBREAD

"Put all your mix in except buttermilk or milk. Use egg nog instead. You will have a very delicious pan of bread."

Bil Curry
Hardin, Texas

SUNDAY BRUNCH CORNBREAD

1 pound bulk pork sausage
2 cups cornbread batter
1 cup grated cheddar cheese
1 cup whole-kernel corn (canned, frozen or fresh)
½ cup finely chopped onion

Cook sausage till done. Drain and crumble; set aside.

In a large mixing bowl, mix 2 cups of your favorite cornbread recipe. Into the cornbread batter, fold the crumbled, cooked sausage (about 2 cups), cheese, corn and onion. Pour mixture into a greased 9 × 13-inch baking dish. Bake at 425° for about 25 minutes or until done.

Cut into serving squares and serve hot. This is a good one-dish casserole. Serve with a fresh fruit salad on the side.

Maggie McDonald
Conroe, Texas

EAST TEXAS HOT-WATER CORNBREAD

2 cups white cornmeal
¾ cup flour
1 teaspoon salt
2 teaspoons baking powder
3 cups boiling water
Cooking oil

Mix dry ingredients well. Stir about 1 cup boiling water into dry mixture. (Set water back on burner to keep it boiling hot.) Pour 1 cup more water into dough while stirring. Dough will begin to swell and become pliable. Pour remaining boiling water into mixture and continue to stir until the dough is well mixed.

Dip hands into cold water and shape small portions of dough into patties or corn sticks. You may vary the sizes of the pieces as desired. Fry in iron skillet. Use a good cooking oil, and heat approximately ⅜-inch of it to medium high before dropping in the corn sticks. Fry brown to taste, turning sticks on all sides while cooking.

Bertie F. Parker
Flatonia, Texas

JULIA BIHL'S HUSH PUPPIES

2 cups cornmeal
1 tablespoon salt
1 tablespoon lard
2 cups boiling water or enough to make a stiff mush

Combine ingredients and shape into rolls or patties, and fry in hot grease to a golden brown.

Barbara Moore
Leander, Texas

"Do you know how 'Hush Puppies' got its name? In pioneer days several families would go to the river and camp overnight to fish. Not even the dogs stayed at home. So when they had fried the fish and the cornbread and eaten all that they wanted while the dogs mournfully howled at the tantalizing smells, they would throw the leftovers to the dogs and say, 'Hush, Puppies.'"

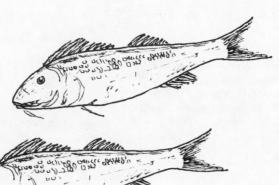

HUSH PUPPIES

1 cup cornmeal
½ cup flour
¼ teaspoon salt
¼ tablespoon baking powder
2 tablespoons sugar
½ cup finely chopped onion
1 egg
½ cup water

Mix ingredients in order given. Drop by teaspoonfuls into hot oil.

Jackie Vanway
Missouri City, Texas

SQUASH PUPPIES

5 medium yellow squash
1 egg, beaten
½ cup buttermilk
1 medium onion, chopped
¾ cup self-rising cornmeal
¼ cup flour

Slice squash. Cover with water and cook over medium heat until done, 15 to 20 minutes. Drain, mash and then drain again. Combine all ingredients. Drop mixture by scant tablespoon into hot peanut oil (350°) for several minutes, until golden brown. Drain on paper towels. Yields about 2½ dozen.

Virginia Austin
Houston, Texas

INDIAN FRY BREAD

3 cups sifted flour
4 teaspoons baking powder
¼ tablespoon salt
Oil for deep frying

"They always have a booth for this at the Livingston Festival each year in October or November and people are lined up, it's so good."

Mix ingredients with sufficient water to make a stiff dough. Place in covered bowl and let sit 30 minutes to an hour. Pinch off small balls of dough and work out into 5-inch circles. (These resemble tortillas but should have a slight depression in the center, for filling.) Fry in deep oil until golden brown. Put a spoonful of beans in the center and top with chopped lettuce, tomatoes and grated cheese.

Debra Ramsden
Huffman, Texas

HERB ROLLS

¼ cup butter or margarine
1½ teaspoons parsley flakes
½ teaspoon dill seed
3 tablespoons Parmesan cheese
1 can refrigerated biscuit dough

Put butter, parsley, dill seed and cheese into a metal 9-inch pie pan. Stir and melt mixture over low heat. Cut each biscuit into quarters and swish each piece in butter mixture. Arrange pieces so they all touch. Bake uncovered 12 to 15 minutes at 425°.

Mary Easley
Rosenberg, Texas

SO-GOOD YEAST ROLLS, PLUS

In addition to the rolls' being so good that they melt in your mouth, the dough can be stored in the refrigerator up to 5 days, letting you enjoy good old yeast rolls for several meals, without the mixing procedure.

2 teaspoons sugar
1 teaspoon salt
2 packages dry yeast
½ cup water
2 eggs
8 cups flour
½ cup sugar
1 cup shortening, melted
1½ cups water

Combine first 5 ingredients in a mixing bowl; set aside. Mix remaining ingredients in a large bowl. Add yeast mixture and combine thoroughly. Let sit in warm place (85°), free from drafts, about 3 hours or until dough has doubled in bulk. Punch dough down. Cover and refrigerate overnight. With lightly floured hands, shape dough into 1½-inch balls; place in 3 greased 9-inch pans. Let dough rise in warm place about 2 hours or until doubled in bulk.

Bake rolls at 400° for 10 to 12 minutes. Yields about 2½ dozen.

Don Kimball
Alvin, Texas

1 TO 3 YEAST DOUGH

In a large bowl mix the following:

1 cup flour
1/3 cup dry milk
3 tablespoons sugar
1 package dry yeast

Stir in 1 cup of lukewarm water and let mixture sit at room temperature. In about ½ to ¾ hour the mixture will become bubbly and will about double in volume. When this happens, add the following:

1 egg
1 teaspoon salt
3 tablespoons shortening

Again mix well, adding flour until the dough is rather thick and will hold its shape. Cover the bowl with a damp cloth and let the dough rise again at room temperature until about doubled in volume. At this time, scrape the dough onto a well-floured pastry cloth. Add flour to the top of the dough and knead it for several minutes, adding more flour as required to the dough and your hands until it is no longer sticky and is workable.

You can now roll the dough out and make any number of bread products—dinner rolls, bread, sweet rolls, doughnuts, etc. After forming dough into desired shape, allow it to rise a third time. Bake it at 350°. For doughnuts, deep-fry in hot shortening.

Lorren F. Bridge
Houston, Texas

SPOON ROLLS

1 package yeast
¼ cup warm water
1 teaspoon sugar
Additional ¼ cup sugar
½ cup shortening, melted
1 teaspoon salt
¾ cup milk
½ cup cold water
3½ cups flour

Dissolve yeast in warm water with 1 teaspoon sugar. In a large bowl blend ¼ cup sugar, shortening and salt. Scald milk and add to the above mixture, then cool by adding the cold water. Add 1 beaten egg (or 2 egg whites). Add dissolved yeast and flour. Blend with a spoon.

Cover and let rise until doubled in bulk, 45 to 60

minutes. Stir down and spoon into well-greased muffin tins, filling half full. Let rise again until dough reaches edge of tins and is rounded in center (about 45 minutes). Bake at 400° for 15 to 20 minutes.

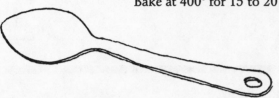

Annie B. Adams
Midland, Texas

JAILHOUSE ROLLS

1 package dry yeast
1½ cups lukewarm water
1 cup mashed potatoes
2 sticks margarine
3 whole eggs
1½ teaspoons salt
1 cup sugar
7 cups flour

"From a jailhouse cook."

Mix dry yeast in lukewarm water; blend. Set aside for later use. Mix potatoes, margarine, eggs, salt and sugar; blend into the flour. Add yeast water, blending well. Place in greased bowl and cover with a damp cloth. Keep in refrigerator until ready for use.

Roll out and cut to desired size. Butter tops and let stand for several hours. Bake at 450° for about 10 minutes.

Faye Boyd
Lake Jackson, Texas

QUICK HOT ROLLS

1 package dry yeast
1 cup warm water
2 tablespoons sugar
2¼ cups flour, unsifted
1 teaspoon salt
2 tablespoons vegetable oil
1 egg

Sprinkle yeast over water in large bowl, stirring until dissolved. Add sugar, half of flour, and salt. Beat well with spoon until smooth and then add egg and oil. Beat in rest of flour until smooth. Scrape down sides of bowl, cover with wet cloth, and let rise in warm place until double (about 50 minutes). Stir down and spoon into 12 lightly greased muffin tins. Let rise about 45 minutes. Bake at 450° about 12 minutes.

Note: The dough will be sticky, but do not add more flour.

Hoytt Jones
Odessa, Texas

HOMEMADE CRACKERS

4 cups flour
1 teaspoon salt
2 tablespoons sugar
¼ cup butter
1 cup milk

Sift dry ingredients into a bowl. Cut in butter until mealy. Stir in milk to make a stiff dough. Roll out on floured surface. Cut into shapes with knife or cookie cutters. Pierce each cracker several times with a fork. Bake on lightly greased cookie sheets until golden brown, about 15 minutes at 400°.

Jane Luttrell
Pasadena, Texas

JANET'S SURPRISE PUMPKIN BREAD

4½ cups sugar
1½ cups cooking oil
6 eggs
2 teaspoons baking powder
2 teaspoons ground nutmeg
1 large can pumpkin (or 3½ cups)
7 cups flour
½ cup Coconut Amaretto liqueur
4 teaspoons baking soda
2¼ teaspoons salt
2 teaspoons ground cloves
4 teaspoons cinnamon
1 12-ounce bag chocolate chips
½ cup chopped pecans
2 teaspoons vanilla

Blend sugar and oil. Add eggs 1 at a time. Add remaining ingredients in order listed. Blend well. Pour into 5 loaf pans that have been greased and floured. Bake 1 hour, 15 minutes at 300° or until done. You must use a large mixing bowl. Loaves may be frozen in Ziploc bags.

Janet Weiton
La Marque, Texas

PERSIMMON BREAD

2 cups flour
2 teaspoons baking powder
½ teaspoon soda
½ teaspoon salt
1 teaspoon cinnamon
½ teaspoon nutmeg
1 cup sugar
1 cup persimmon pulp
½ cup milk
2 eggs, slightly beaten
¼ cup butter, softened
1 cup chopped walnuts or pecans

Combine flour, baking powder, soda, salt, cinnamon and nutmeg, and stir lightly. Set aside. Combine sugar, persimmon pulp, milk, eggs and butter; mix well. Add dry ingredients to this mixture. Mix well. Stir in nuts. Spoon batter into a greased and floured loaf pan. Bake at 350° for 45 minutes or until bread tests done. Yields 1 loaf.

Lucille Meredith
Elgin, Texas

STRAWBERRY BREAD

3 cups all-purpose flour
1 teaspoon soda
½ teaspoon salt
1 teaspoon cinnamon
2 cups sugar
3 eggs, beaten
1 cup vegetable oil
2 or 3 10-ounce packages frozen sliced strawberries, thawed

Combine first 5 ingredients, mixing well. Combine eggs and oil and some of strawberry juice. Add to dry ingredients, mixing well. Add remainder of strawberries.

Pour batter into 2 greased and floured 9 × 5 × 3-inch loaf pans. Bake at 350° for 1 hour or until wooden pick inserted in center comes out clean. Cool in pan 10 minutes.

Marie Allen
Houston, Texas

RAISIN BREAD

2 cups boiling water
1 pound raisins
2 teaspoons baking soda
½ cup butter
2 cups sugar
2 eggs, lightly beaten
4 cups flour
2 teaspoons cinnamon
1 teaspoon salt
½ cup pecans

Pour boiling water over raisins, baking soda and butter. Let stand to cool. Add remaining ingredients and mix well. Pour batter into 3 greased 9-inch square pans. Bake for 1 hour or until done at 350°. Let sit 10 minutes before removing from pans.

Grace Campbell
Llano, Texas

POPPY-SEED BREAD

1 package white cake mix
1 small box vanilla instant pudding
¼ cup poppy seeds
4 eggs
½ cup oil
1 cup hot water

Combine all ingredients and beat for 4 minutes. Pour into 2 greased and floured loaf pans and bake 50 minutes at 350°.

Marjorie McIntosh
Houston, Texas

BUTTER-SCOTCH BANANA BREAD

1¾ cups flour
2 teaspoons baking powder
½ teaspoon baking soda
½ teaspoon cinnamon
½ teaspoon nutmeg
½ teaspoon salt
1 cup mashed banana (2 medium bananas)
¾ cup sugar
2 eggs
¼ cup melted butter
¼ cup milk
1 cup chopped pecans
1 6-ounce package butterscotch morsels
⅓ cup pecan pieces

Sift together the first 6 ingredients; set aside. Combine bananas, sugar, eggs and melted butter. Blend well. Alternately blend dry ingredients and milk into the banana mixture. Stir in the chopped pecans and butterscotch morsels.

Pour into greased 9 × 5 × 3-inch loaf pan. Sprinkle pecan pieces on top. Bake at 350° for about 1 hour. Cool 30 minutes, then remove from pan. Yields 1 loaf.

Fairy Wagner
Spring, Texas

BROWN BREAD

"This 100-year-old recipe is really good for making cream-cheese or ham sandwiches, or with just plain butter."

1½ cups buttermilk
⅓ cup molasses or honey in cup
Enough sugar to fill balance of cup
3 cups stone-ground wheat flour
1 teaspoon soda
1 teaspoon salt
½ to 1 cup raisins (optional)

Put buttermilk, molasses and sugar in bowl, and stir gently. Add flour, soda and salt. Stir very little (only until flour is mixed well). Add raisins (if desired).

Grease bread pan, and flour with wheat flour. Cook at 350° for about 1 hour. Butter outside of cooked loaf while hot and wrap tightly in wax paper and let steam until cool.

Helen Byrne
Houston, Texas

QUICK BROWN BREAD

"This is good with baked beans, but it is also good the next day served with butter and something hot. It is even good dunked in coffee."

1½ cups flour
2½ teaspoons baking soda
1½ teaspoons salt
¼ cup sugar
2 cups whole-wheat flour
⅓ cup shortening
1 egg, well beaten
2 cups buttermilk
¾ cup molasses or cane syrup

Sift flour, soda, salt and sugar together. Stir in whole-wheat flour and mix well. Cut in shortening until mixture resembles coarse meal.

Combine egg, buttermilk and molasses. Add to dry

ingredients. Mix until all flour is dampened. Do not over-mix.

Pour into 2 greased and floured loaf pans. Bake in a 350° oven for 45 to 50 minutes. Best served hot.

Jeannette Werner
Santa Fe, Texas

SOFT GINGERBREAD

1 cup molasses
½ cup sugar
8 tablespoons shortening or butter
1 teaspoon soda dissolved in ½ cup water
2½ cups flour
1 teaspoon ginger
½ teaspoon cloves
2 teaspoons cinnamon
2 teaspoons baking powder

Combine first 4 ingredients. Sift dry ingredients and add to first mixture. Beat hard to blend, and then pour into well-greased and floured pan and bake in a slow oven for 35 minutes.

Orine Hoag
Austin, Texas

"This recipe is from a cookbook that my Mother got in 1918 when she was sixteen years old. I still have the book."

GRANDMA SWEARIN-GEN'S DELICIOUS GINGERBREAD

1 cup sugar
1 cup vegetable oil
1 cup ribbon cane syrup
2 eggs
2 cups flour
1 teaspoon soda
Pinch of salt
2 teaspoons nutmeg
2 teaspoons cinnamon
2 teaspoons ginger
1 cup buttermilk
1 tablespoon vinegar

Mix first 4 ingredients. Mix flour, soda, salt and spices. Combine with first mixture. Add buttermilk and vinegar. Mix and bake at 350° for 30 minutes in greased and floured 10 × 14-inch baking pan.

Mrs. Leon Sitton
Nacogdoches, Texas

BEER BREAD

1 can beer
3 cups self-rising flour
3 tablespoons sugar
Melted butter

Pour beer slowly into flour and sugar. Mix well with a spoon. Pour into an ungreased loaf pan. Bake in 350° oven approximately 25 minutes or until a straw comes out clean. Baste top with butter. The bread may be baked in an outdoor covered grill if the temperature is kept on low.

Robert Egleston
Needville, Texas

GREEK BREAD

1 stick margarine, softened
½ cup mayonnaise
1 or 2 green onions, chopped fine
Garlic to taste
½ cup chopped black olives
3 ounces shredded mozzarella cheese
1 large loaf French bread

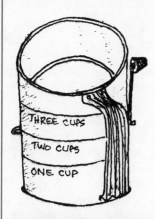

Blend margarine and mayonnaise. Add onions, garlic, olives, and cheese. Split loaf of French bread and spread mixture evenly on both sides. Close and wrap. Refrigerate for 24 hours or overnight. When ready to serve, open and respread. Bake in 350° oven for 15 to 20 minutes.

Petty Schoelman
Houston, Texas

SWEDISH RYE BREAD

1 package yeast
2½ cups lukewarm water, divided
½ cup shortening
¾ cup sugar (¼ brown)
½ cup molasses
1 tablespoon salt
1 teaspoon anise seed
2 tablespoons caraway seed
1 teaspoon finely grated orange peel
6 cups white flour, divided
1 cup rye flour

Dissolve yeast in ½ cup lukewarm water. Mix 2 cups water with shortening, sugar, molasses, salt and seeds. Add yeast mixture. Add orange peel, rye flour and 3 cups white flour. Mix well. Cover with cloth and let rise until double in bulk. Add 3 more cups white flour and knead for several minutes. Let rise until double in bulk. Make into 2 loaves. Put in greased bread pans. Let rise again until double. Bake 35 to 40 minutes at 350°. When bread is done, wipe tops with wet cloth to keep top from being too crusty.

Adelien Rosprim
Austin, Texas

RYE BREAD

¼ cup brown sugar
¼ cup light molasses
1 tablespoon salt
2 tablespoons shortening
1½ cups, boiling water
1 package active dry yeast
¼ cup warm water (110° to 115°)
2½ cups rye flour
2 tablespoons grated orange peel
3½ to 4 cups all-purpose flour

Combine brown sugar, molasses, salt and shortening in large bowl; pour on boiling water and stir until sugar is dissolved. Cool to lukewarm.

Sprinkle yeast on warm water; stir to dissolve.

Stir rye flour into brown sugar–molasses mixture, beating well. Stir in yeast and orange peel; beat until smooth.

Mix in enough of the flour, a little at a time, to make a smooth, soft dough. Turn onto lightly floured board or pastry cloth; knead until satiny and elastic, about 10 minutes. Place dough in lightly greased bowl; turn dough over to grease top. Cover and let rise in warm place until dough is doubled, 1½ to 2 hours.

Punch down; turn dough onto lightly floured pastry cloth and divide in half. Round up dough to make 2 balls. Cover and let rest 10 minutes. Shape into loaves and place in 2 greased 9 × 5 × 3-inch loaf pans. Cover and let rise in a warm place until almost doubled, 1½ to 2 hours.

Bake at 375° for 25 to 30 minutes, covering with foil the last 15 minutes if loaves are browning too fast. Turn onto wire racks to cool. Brush with melted butter while warm if you like a soft crust. Yields 2 loaves.

Ruby Schafer
Houston, Texas

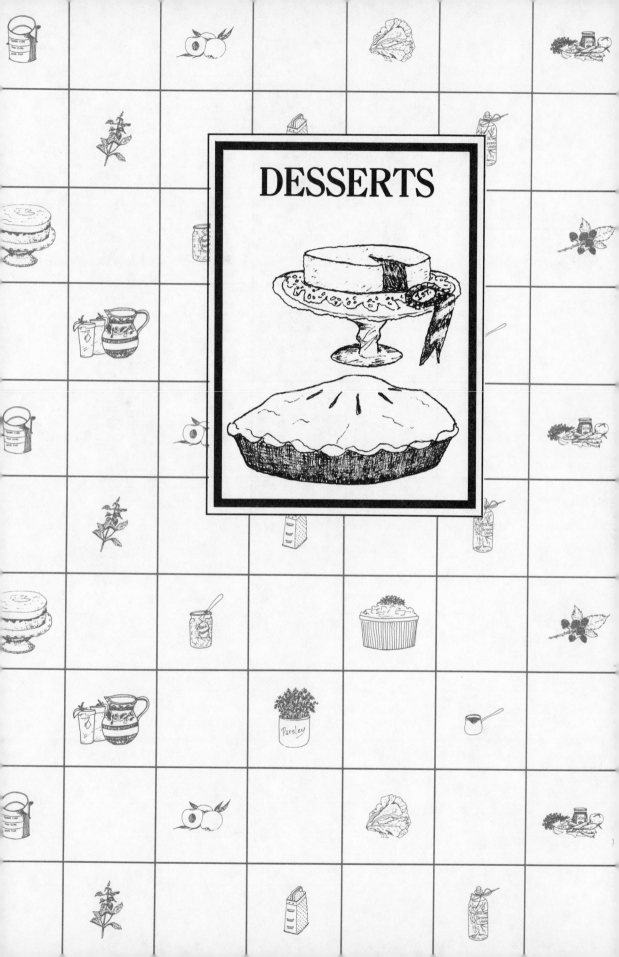

DESSERTS

CAKES

GERMAN FRUITCAKE

2 cups sugar
1 cup butter
4 eggs
2¼ cups flour
1 teaspoon soda
½ teaspoon cinnamon
½ teaspoon nutmeg
½ cup cocoa
1½ cups chopped pecans
1 cup raisins
1 cup buttermilk

"This recipe has been in my family over sixty years. I grew up on a small ranch in San Saba County near the town of Pontotoc. This recipe was given to my oldest sister and was made for Christmas and considered a delicacy. We always had plenty of milk, butter and eggs."

Cream sugar and butter. Beat in eggs 1 at a time. Sift together the flour, soda, cinnamon, nutmeg and cocoa. Dredge pecans and raisins in flour mixture. Mix all ingredients, including buttermilk, in a large bowl. Bake in layers at 350° for 30 minutes. Frost when layers are cool.

FROSTING:
2 cups sugar
1 cup milk
3 tablespoons molasses
Butter the size of a walnut
½ teaspoon vanilla

Boil first 3 ingredients until a drop placed in cold water forms a soft ball. Remove from heat and beat, adding butter and vanilla.

Margaret Johnson
Rosenberg, Texas

SMALL FRUITCAKE

1½ cups sugar
½ cup butter
1 8-ounce can crushed pineapple
1 cup raisins
1 cup pecans
1 cup pitted cherries
3 cups flour
1 teaspoon cloves
½ teaspoon nutmeg
½ teaspoon salt
1 teaspoon soda dissolved in ¼ cup boiling water

"This recipe is over sixty years old and makes a very simple and good-tasting cake."

Cream sugar and butter. Stir fruit and nuts into mixture. Sift dry ingredients and blend into fruit mixture. Add soda dissolved in water. Bake in a prepared loaf or tube pan at 350° for 1 hour.

Annie Socha
El Campo, Texas

MINCEMEAT FRUITCAKE

2¼ cups sifted all-purpose flour
1½ teaspoons baking powder
½ teaspoon soda
½ teaspoon salt
½ cup butter
1 cup sugar
2 eggs
1 1-pound jar mincemeat
½ cup apple butter
1 cup chopped nuts
1 teaspoon vanilla

"I bake this cake every Christmas, as our family likes it better than the usual fruitcake. It will stay fresh and moist a long time."

Sift together the flour, baking powder, soda and salt, and set aside. Cream butter and sugar thoroughly. Add eggs 1 at a time, beating well after each. Stir in mincemeat, apple butter, nuts and vanilla. Add dry ingredients, mixing well. Pour into greased tube pan. Bake at 325° for 1½ hours. Cake does not need to age before serving.

Mrs. J. W. Thornton
Dickinson, Texas

PEAR CAKE

4 cups thinly sliced pears
1 cup chopped pecans
2 cups sugar
3 cups flour
½ teaspoon salt
½ teaspoon cinnamon
½ teaspoon nutmeg
½ teaspoon allspice
½ teaspoon soda
1 cup white raisins
2 eggs, beaten
1 cup cooking oil
1 teaspoon vanilla
3 teaspoons rum

Mix pears, pecans and sugar, and let stand 1 hour (never less than 30 minutes). Sift together the flour, salt, spices and soda, and set aside. To the pear mixture add raisins, eggs, oil, vanilla and rum. Stir in the dry ingredients. Mix well. Grease and flour a tube or loaf pan. Bake 1 to 1½ hours, depending on oven, at 350°.

Marye Krause
Bellaire, Texas

OLD-FASHIONED PRUNE CAKE

1 cup sugar
¾ cup shortening
3 eggs
½ cup sour cream
1 cup cooked chopped prunes
2 cups flour
2 teaspoons baking powder
1 teaspoon soda
2 teaspoons cinnamon
1 teaspoon allspice
1 teaspoon cloves
Dash of salt
1 cup pecans

Cream together the sugar and shortening. Add eggs, beating till smooth. Add sour cream and prunes. Sift together dry ingredients. Add to first mixture and mix until smooth. Do not beat. Stir in pecans.

Divide mixture into 3 greased and floured 9-inch cake

pans. Bake in preheated 350° oven 30 to 40 minutes. Cake is done when center springs back when touched. Cool on wire rack.

ICING:
2 eggs
½ cup sour cream
1 cup cooked chopped prunes
2 tablespoons butter or margarine
Walnut halves for garnish

Combine ingredients (except nuts) in a 3-quart saucepan. Cook over medium heat, stirring constantly until thick. Spread over the cake layers and garnish top with walnut halves or pecans.

Frankie Franks
Deer Park, Texas

TEXAS APPLE CAKE

3 cups flour
2 cups sugar
2 teaspoons baking soda
1 teaspoon salt
1½ cups cooking oil
2 eggs
3 teaspoons lemon juice
3 tablespoons vanilla
4 medium apples, peeled, cored and sliced thin
1 cup chopped pecans

Mix first 8 ingredients in order listed. Fold in the apples and pecans. (This cake mixture will resemble cookie dough.) Pat down in lightly greased and floured 13 × 9-inch pan. Bake at 325° for 50 minutes. Ice with Cream-Cheese Frosting.

"This recipe has been passed from one neighbor to the other for so long I can't remember where it started. It has to be the best apple cake in Texas."

CREAM-CHEESE FROSTING:
2 cups powdered sugar
1 stick softened margarine or butter
1 8-ounce package cream cheese, softened
1 teaspoon vanilla

Blend ingredients well and spread on cooled cake. Top with additional chopped pecans, if desired.

Giorgia Brandt
Houston, Texas

FRESH APPLE CAKE

6 apples, peeled and grated
2 cups sugar
1 cup chopped pecans
2 eggs, beaten
2 teaspoons vanilla
1 cup vegetable oil
3 cups flour
½ teaspoon salt
2 teaspoons soda
1 teaspoon cinnamon

Preheat oven to 350°. Mix apples, sugar and pecans, and let stand 1 hour, stirring often. Add eggs, vanilla and oil. Sift all other ingredients together and add to the first mixture. Pour into a large tube pan that has been greased and floured. Bake 1 hour and 15 minutes.

Ruth Talafuse
Wharton, Texas

FIG CAKE

2½ cups chopped figs
3 cups flour
1 teaspoon baking powder
1½ teaspoons soda
1 teaspoon cinnamon
1 teaspoon nutmeg
1 teaspoon allspice
1½ cups pecans
½ teaspoon salt
2 teaspoons vanilla
1 cup vegetable oil
3 eggs
3 cups sugar
2 to 4 teaspoons rum

"I have to bake this cake every year for the Bellaire Antiques Fair because people always come around asking for it."

Cook whole figs in a little water and sugar about 15 minutes before chopping. Blend next 8 ingredients and set aside. Mix figs, vanilla, oil, eggs and rum. Mix well. Add sugar, stirring until syrupy. Add to dry ingredients. If too thin or moist, add ¼ cup flour. Put in lightly greased and floured bundt pan or 2 small loaf pans. Bake for about 50 minutes to 1 hour at 350°.

Marye Krause
Bellaire, Texas

PINEAPPLE UPSIDE-DOWN CAKE

1 cup crushed pineapple, drained
1 cup brown sugar
3 tablespoons butter

Cook all together in saucepan until sugar is dissolved. Butter 2 round cake tins thoroughly; add pineapple mixture, half in each tin. Place 5 or 6 maraschino cherries in each tin. While this mixture is cooling in the cake tins, mix the following batter.

½ cup butter
1 cup sugar
2 egg yolks, beaten
2½ teaspoons baking powder
2 cups flour
½ cup milk
1 teaspoon vanilla
2 egg whites, stiffly beaten

Cream butter, add sugar gradually and beat until light. Add beaten egg yolks and mix thoroughly. Sift baking powder and flour together 3 times and add alternately with milk. Add vanilla and carefully fold in stiffly beaten whites. Pour this batter over pineapple mixture, half in each tin, being careful not to disturb the cherries. Bake at 400° for 25 minutes. Cool for a few minutes. Invert tins. Serve with whipped cream.

(Fern Minear Devlin)
Barbara Moore
Leander, Texas

PINEAPPLE SURPRISE CAKE

This cake is very easy and quick to make. It also freezes well for serving at a later date.

1 egg, beaten
2 cups sugar
2 cups flour
2 teaspoons baking soda
1 20-ounce can crushed pineapple, including juice
1 teaspoon vanilla
½ cup chopped nuts
¼ teaspoon salt

To beaten egg, add sugar and beat till well mixed. Sift flour and soda together and add to sugar mixture. Add remaining ingredients and mix thoroughly. Pour into greased and floured sheet-cake pan. Bake 30 to 35 minutes at 350°. Be sure center of cake is springy to touch before removing from oven. Ice cake while it is warm.

ICING:
1 8-ounce package cream cheese, at room temperature
½ stick margarine, softened
1¾ cups powdered sugar
1 teaspoon vanilla
½ cup chopped nuts

Beat cream cheese and margarine together. Sift in the powdered sugar and beat till smooth. Add vanilla and nuts, mixing well. Spread on warm cake.

Yvonne York
Pasadena, Texas

FRUIT COCKTAIL CAKE

1½ cups sugar
2 teaspoons soda
Pinch of salt
2 cups flour
2 well-beaten eggs
1 17-ounce can fruit cocktail, drained (save juice)

Combine sugar, soda, salt and flour. Add eggs and juice from fruit cocktail. Mix well and add fruit cocktail. Bake in lightly greased and floured sheet pan at 350° for 35 to 40 minutes. Ice while still hot.

ICING:
¾ cup sugar
½ cup evaporated milk
1 stick margarine
1 teaspoon vanilla
½ cup coconut

Cook sugar, milk and margarine for 2 minutes. Then add vanilla and coconut. Mix well and spread on cake.

Anne Lytle
Dayton, Texas

PUMPKIN DESSERT RING

1⅔ cups sifted flour
1⅓ cups sugar
¼ teaspoon baking powder
1 teaspoon soda
¾ teaspoon salt
½ teaspoon cinnamon
¼ teaspoon cloves
⅓ cup soft shortening
⅓ cup water
⅓ cup chopped nuts
⅔ cup raisins
1 cup pumpkin
1 large unbeaten egg

Heat oven to 350°. Grease well a 2-quart ring mold. Sift dry ingredients; add shortening, water, nuts, raisins and pumpkin. Beat 2 minutes at medium speed with electric mixer. Add egg, beating 2 minutes more. Pour in mold and bake 40 to 45 minutes. It will have a "pudding" part near the bottom.

Betty Pecore
Austin, Texas

PUMPKIN CAKE

3 cups flour
2 teaspoons baking powder
2 teaspoons soda
1 teaspoon salt
1 teaspoon cinnamon
1 teaspoon nutmeg
1 teaspoon allspice
½ teaspoon cloves
4 eggs, beaten
2 cups sugar
2 cups pumpkin, canned or fresh pureed
1¼ cups vegetable oil
1 cup chopped nuts

Sift flour, baking powder, soda, salt and spices together. Blend eggs and sugar; add pumpkin and oil. Add flour mixture and nuts. Bake in tube pan 1 hour at 350°. Seal in airtight container while cake is warm, for a really moist cake.

Lucille Foster
Lake Jackson, Texas

AUNT LARONA'S RAISIN CAKE

1½ cups raisins
1 cup water
¼ cup shortening
¾ cup sugar
1 egg
1⅔ cups sifted flour
1 teaspoon soda
¼ teaspoon salt
¼ teaspoon cloves
½ teaspoon cinnamon
½ teaspoon allspice
1 teaspoon vanilla

Simmer raisins in water until tender. Drain, reserving ½ cup of the liquid. Cream shortening and sugar together. Add egg, beating well. Sift together dry ingredients. Add to creamed mixture alternately with the ½ cup raisin water. Add vanilla. Mix only until smooth, and stir in the raisins.

Pour into a greased and floured oblong baking pan. Bake at 350° for 40 to 45 minutes. Watch that the raisins on top don't burn at the last. A piece of foil laid over the top will prevent this. Cool for 10 minutes and turn out. Frost with a butter icing.

Betty Pecore
Austin, Texas

WHITE RAISIN CAKE

1 pound butter
2 cups sugar
6 eggs
3½ cups flour
1 teaspoon baking powder
Pinch of salt
4 cups chopped pecans
1 16-ounce box white raisins, dredged in flour
2 ounces lemon extract

Mix all ingredients in order listed. Place in prepared loaf pan and bake 2½ hours at 250°.

Mrs. Oran Standley
Nacogdoches, Texas

OLD-FASHIONED CHERRY-NUT CAKE

2¼ cups flour
1⅓ cups sugar
3 teaspoons baking powder
½ teaspoon salt
½ cup shortening
¼ cup maraschino-cherry juice
16 chopped maraschino cherries
½ cup milk
½ to ⅔ cup unbeaten egg whites
½ cup chopped pecans

Sift together the first 4 ingredients. Add shortening, cherry juice, cherries and milk. Beat well for 10 minutes. Add eggs and pecans and mix well. Pour into a greased and floured oblong pan. Bake at 350° for 35 minutes. Cool and spread with icing.

ICING:
1 box powdered sugar
½ cup melted butter
2 tablespoons milk
2 tablespoons maraschino-cherry juice
10 chopped maraschino cherries
½ cup chopped pecans

Mix ingredients until smooth, and spread on cool cake.

Mrs. Eston Harrington
Dayton, Texas

CARROT CAKE

4 eggs
2 cups sugar
1½ cups vegetable oil
2 cups flour
1 teaspoon salt
1½ teaspoons baking soda
2 teaspoons cinnamon
2 cups grated carrots

Cream together the eggs, sugar and oil. Add dry ingredients and mix well. Add grated carrots, stirring well to blend. Pour batter into a greased and floured 9 × 13-inch pan. Bake at 375° for 35 minutes. When cooled, ice with Cream-Cheese Frosting.

CREAM-CHEESE FROSTING:
½ stick butter
4 ounces cream cheese, softened
8 ounces powdered sugar
1 teaspoon vanilla extract
1 cup broken pecans

Cream butter and cream cheese. Add sugar and vanilla. Mix well. Add pecans. Spread evenly over cake.

Lenee MacDonald
Romayor, Texas

HARVEST PECAN CAKE

4½ cups sifted flour
¼ teaspoon salt
1 teaspoon baking powder
2 cups margarine, softened
1 pound brown sugar
6 egg yolks
½ cup milk
1 teaspoon vanilla
3 tablespoons instant coffee, dissolved in 3 tablespoons hot water
4 cups chopped pecans
1 cup raisins (optional)
6 egg whites, beaten

Sift together flour, salt and baking powder. In large mixing bowl, cream together margarine and brown sugar. Add beaten egg yolks and mix well. Combine milk, vanilla and dissolved coffee. Add milk mixture and dry ingredients alternately into creamed mixture. Fold in pecans, raisins and egg whites. Pour into greased and floured tube or bundt pan. Bake at 350° for 1½ hours. Let cool in pan on rack. Remove from pan. Serve as is or with Whipped Cream Imperial.

WHIPPED CREAM IMPERIAL:
1 cup whipping cream
⅛ teaspoon salt
½ teaspoon vanilla
½ cup sieved brown sugar (do not pack)

Beat all ingredients until stiff.

Shirley Wylie
Livingston, Texas

TEXAS PECAN TORTE

2 cups ground pecans
2 tablespoons flour
1 cup sugar
4 eggs, separated, plus 1 whole egg

Grind nuts. Mix with 2 tablespoons flour. Beat sugar with egg yolks and 1 whole egg until pale, and mix into nuts and flour. Beat egg whites until stiff; fold into sugar-egg mixture. Pour into 3 greased and lined 9-inch pans. Bake at 350° for 15 to 20 minutes. Cake will spring back to touch when done. Remove from pans immediately after taking from oven.

FILLING:
2 cups heavy cream
3 tablespoons powdered sugar
1 teaspoon vanilla

Whip ingredients together until thick. Divide between pecan layers.

ICING:
8 ounces semisweet chocolate
3 tablespoons unsalted butter
¼ cup sour cream
Chopped pecans

Melt together chocolate and butter. Remove from heat. Stir in sour cream or crème fraîche. Let cool until thick enough to spread. Ice cake, then press chopped pecans around side.

Mary Kuess
Austin, Texas

GRANDMA EGLESTON'S PRIZE-WINNING NUT TORTE

5 eggs, separated
1 cup sugar
1 cup sifted flour
1 teaspoon baking powder
5 tablespoons water
1 teaspoon vanilla
½ teaspoon salt
1 cup ground walnuts

Beat yolks until lemon-colored; add sugar and beat well. Add flour, baking powder, water, vanilla and salt, mixing well. Beat egg whites until stiff, fold egg whites into above mixture, and add nuts. Place in 2 prepared 9-inch layer pans. Bake at 350° for 25 to 30 minutes.

BUTTERCREAM ICING:
1 small package vanilla pudding (not instant)
1 cup milk
½ cup shortening
½ cup butter
1 cup sugar
1 teaspoon vanilla
Ground nuts

Make vanilla pudding with 1 cup milk; cook and cool. Combine shortening, butter, sugar and vanilla, and beat well, then add to cooled pudding. Spread between cooled layers and on top of cake. Sprinkle with ground nuts.

Marilyn Egleston
Needville, Texas

SOUR CREAM POUND CAKE

2¾ cups sugar
1 cup butter or margarine
6 eggs
3 cups sifted all-purpose flour
½ teaspoon salt (optional)
¼ teaspoon baking soda
1 cup sour cream
½ teaspoon lemon extract
½ teaspoon orange extract
½ teaspoon almond extract
1 teaspoon vanilla extract

In mixer bowl, cream together sugar and butter until light and fluffy. Add eggs 1 at a time, beating well after each addition. Sift together dry ingredients and add to creamed mixture alternately with sour cream, beating well after each addition. Add extracts; beat well.

Pour into greased and lightly floured 10-inch tube pan. Bake in 325° oven about 1 hour 40 minutes or until cake tests done. Cool 15 minutes, then remove from pan. When cool, sprinkle with powdered sugar, if desired.

Roberta Rogers
Midland, Texas

MY GRANDMA LAMAR'S POUND CAKE

"This recipe has been in my family for over seventy-five years. The flavor and texture of this cake are different."

10 eggs, separated
1 pound butter
2¼ cups sugar
4¼ cups flour
¼ cup whiskey (this is a must)

Beat egg whites and set aside. Cream butter and sugar, add egg yolks, and beat well. Add flour and whiskey and beat well. Add the egg whites last, then beat on medium speed of mixer for about 5 minutes. Bake in 2 greased and floured loaf pans at 300° for about 2 hours.

Peggy McDonald
Big Spring, Texas

BUTTER-RUM POUND CAKE

1 cup shortening
3 cups sugar
6 eggs
3 cups sifted flour
1 teaspoon soda
½ teaspoon salt
1 cup buttermilk
1½ teaspoons butter extract
1½ teaspoons rum extract

Cream shortening, gradually adding sugar until fluffy. Add eggs, one at a time, blending after each addition. Beat for 8 minutes with mixer at medium speed. Sift flour, soda, salt. Add to shortening, sugar, egg mixture, alternately with 1 cup buttermilk. Stir in flavorings. Add a few drops of food coloring for brightness, if desired. Bake at 325° in prepared 10-inch tube pan for 1½ hours, or until tests done.

RUM GLAZE:
¼ cup butter, melted
⅓ cup milk
1 box sifted powdered sugar
1½ teaspoons rum flavoring
1 teaspoon nutmeg

Mix butter, milk and sugar. Stir in rum flavoring and nutmeg. Glaze cake while it is hot.

Dorothy Bookout
Houston, Texas

BUTTERMILK POUND CAKE

3 cups sugar
1 cup shortening
6 eggs, separated
2 teaspoons lemon or orange extract
3 cups flour
½ teaspoon salt
¼ teaspoon baking soda
1 cup buttermilk

Blend sugar and shortening in electric mixer bowl. Add egg yolks, beating well. Add flavoring. Sift dry ingredients together and add to sugar mixture alternately with buttermilk, ending with flour. Beat egg whites until stiff and carefully fold into mixture. Pour batter into greased and floured 10-inch tube pan. Bake in preheated 350° oven for 1 hour and 10 minutes, or until toothpick comes out clean.

Dorothy Bookout
Houston, Texas

CREAM-CHEESE POUND CAKE

3 sticks softened butter or margarine
8 ounces softened cream cheese
3 cups sugar
1½ teaspoons vanilla
3 cups sifted flour
6 large eggs

Cream butter and cream cheese together. On low speed, add remaining ingredients and mix well. Fill greased and floured tube pan and place in unheated oven. Bake at 300° for 90 minutes. Cool 30 minutes on rack, then remove from pan.

Linda Gibson
Kingwood, Texas

EMMA PARVIN'S LEMON POUND CAKE

1 cup shortening
2 cups sugar
4 egg yolks, beaten
3 cups flour
½ teaspoon salt
¼ teaspoon soda
1 cup buttermilk
½ teaspoon lemon extract
4 egg whites, beaten

"This pound cake was my grandmother's. I like it because it can be iced or topped with strawberries or used plain and toasted with butter for breakfast."

Cream shortening, then add sugar and beaten egg yolks. Sift flour with salt. Dissolve soda in buttermilk. Add buttermilk and flour alternately to shortening and sugar. Stir in lemon extract. Beat egg whites until fairly stiff and fold into batter. Bake for 1 hour at 350° in greased and floured tube pan.

Linda Gibson
Kingwood, Texas

DATE LOAF CAKE

2 pounds dates
4 cups pecans
1 pound candied cherries
1 cup flour
1 cup sugar
2 teaspoons baking powder
1 teaspoon salt
4 eggs, separated
1 teaspoon vanilla

Mix dates, pecans and cherries in a large bowl. They may be left whole if desired. Sift dry ingredients together 3 times, sifting over fruit and nut mixture the last time. Add beaten egg yolks; fold or work in stiffly beaten egg whites to which vanilla has been added. Let stand 30 minutes and mix again.

Grease loaf pan, and line with greased wax paper. Cover top of cake with wax paper, and place pan of water under cake. Bake at 250° for 2 hours. Remove cover from top of cake during last 15 minutes of baking. After cake is removed from oven, cool in paper in which it was baked. Wrap in second layer of waxed paper.

Lucinda Hornsby
Pflugerville, Texas

HOT MILK CAKE

1 stick butter
1 cup milk
4 eggs
2 cups sugar
2 cups flour
2 teaspoons baking powder
½ teaspoon salt
¼ cup Mexican vanilla
3 tablespoons corn oil

"This cake won a blue ribbon at the Kenefick Kaper's Fire Department Benefit in 1985 as a pound cake."

Melt butter in milk and set aside. Beat eggs and add sugar, beating until sugar is dissolved. Add flour, baking powder and salt, and beat well on high speed. Add vanilla and oil. Reheat milk mixture until it comes to a boil. Pour into flour mixture and beat on medium speed. Mixture will be very thin.

Bake in a well-greased and floured tube pan for about 45 minutes in a 325° oven. When done, cool on rack 10 to 15 minutes, then turn out on cloth and then on serving plate.

Variation: For a chocolate cake, add 6 tablespoons cocoa to flour.

Lucille Haynes
Dayton, Texas

JELLY ROLL

4 eggs
1 cup sugar
1½ teaspoons vanilla
1 cup flour
½ teaspoon soda
1 teaspoon cream of tartar

Beat eggs until fluffy. Add sugar and vanilla. Stir in flour, soda and cream of tartar. Spread thin on a long tin that has been lined with wax paper. Bake at 350° until done. Turn from tin, cool, spread with jelly, and roll.

Edna Coleman
La Marque, Texas

GERMAN CHOCOLATE CAKE

1 package German's sweet chocolate
½ cup boiling water
2 cups sugar
1 cup shortening
4 eggs, separated
1 cup buttermilk
2½ cups all-purpose flour
1 teaspoon baking soda
½ teaspoon salt
1 tablespoon vanilla

"This cake is a lot of work but is worth it when it comes to 'eating time.'"

Dissolve chocolate in boiling water. Cream sugar and shortening. Add egg yolks 1 at a time and beat thoroughly each time. Add ¾ cup of buttermilk alternately with flour. Add soda to remaining ¼ cup buttermilk and salt. Add chocolate mixture and vanilla. Mix well. Fold in stiffly beaten egg whites. Pour into 2 greased and floured 10-inch cake pans. Bake at 350° for 40 to 45 minutes. Makes two 10-inch layers or three 8-inch layers.

FROSTING:
1 cup sugar
3 egg yolks
1 cup evaporated milk
¼ teaspoon salt
1 teaspoon vanilla
1 cup coconut
1 cup chopped pecans

Mix sugar, egg yolks, evaporated milk, salt and vanilla in top of double boiler, and cook until thick. Add coconut and pecans, and spread on top and between layers. Do not put on sides of cake.

Myrtle Hudgins
Baytown, Texas

ELIZABETH DANIEL'S CHOCOLATE CAKE

4 squares unsweetened chocolate
½ cup butter
1 cup water
2 cups cake flour
2 cups sugar
1½ teaspoons soda
¼ teaspoon salt
¼ teaspoon cream of tartar
½ cup buttermilk
2 eggs
1 teaspoon vanilla

"This is a chocolate-lover's cake. The recipe is from my personal collection, and I am a sixth-generation Texan."

Melt together first 3 ingredients. Do not boil. Sift together dry ingredients. Mix together chocolate mixture and dry ingredients, adding buttermilk. Beat in whole eggs and add vanilla. Bake for 30 minutes at 350° in 2 prepared 9-inch round cake pans.

CHOCOLATE FROSTING:
4 squares unsweetened chocolate
¼ cup water (or less)
1 box powdered sugar
1 egg
1 stick butter, softened
1 teaspoon vanilla

Melt chocolate and water. Add to powdered sugar, egg and butter. Add vanilla. Mix well. Now spread on cake and get fat!

Zia Crowell Miller
Victoria, Texas

FUDGE CAKE

1 cup shortening
2 cups sugar
4 eggs, well beaten
2 cups flour
6 tablespoons cocoa
Pinch of salt
1 teaspoon vanilla
1 cup chopped pecans

Cream shortening and sugar. Add eggs and beat well. Add remaining ingredients. Bake in a greased and floured 9 × 13-inch pan at 325° for 40 minutes.

ICING:
1½ sticks margarine
12 tablespoons milk
8 tablespoons cocoa
1½ boxes powdered sugar
Pinch of salt
2 teaspoons vanilla

Mix margarine, milk and cocoa in a large saucepan, and bring to a boil. Add powdered sugar, salt and vanilla. Mix well. Ice cooled cake and cut into squares.

Bobbie Dykes
Bay City, Texas

HOT FUDGE CAKE

2 cups sugar
2 cups flour
1 stick margarine
½ cup shortening
4 tablespoons cocoa
1 cup water
2 eggs
1 teaspoon soda
½ cup buttermilk
1 teaspoon cinnamon
1 teaspoon vanilla

Mix sugar and flour in bowl. In a saucepan combine margarine, shortening, cocoa and water. Bring to boil and pour over dry ingredients. Add eggs and mix well. Add soda to buttermilk and mix in. Add cinnamon and vanilla. Mix well.

Bake in a greased and floured 9 × 13-inch pan 25 to 30 minutes at 400°. Ice with Hot Fudge Icing while cake is still hot.

HOT FUDGE ICING:
1 stick margarine
4 tablespoons cocoa
6 tablespoons milk
1 box powdered sugar
1 teaspoon vanilla
1 cup pecans

In saucepan mix margarine, cocoa and milk. Bring to boil and pour over powdered sugar. Mix well. Add vanilla and nuts.

Shirley Wylie
Livingston, Texas

OLD-FASHIONED MILK-CHOCOLATE CAKE

2 cups sugar
1 cup shortening
2 eggs, beaten
2 cups buttermilk
3½ cups flour
2 teaspoons soda
4 tablespoons plus 1 teaspoon cocoa
2 teaspoons vanilla

Cream sugar and shortening. Add eggs and beat well. Alternately add buttermilk with sifted dry ingredients. Add vanilla and beat well.

Bake in 3 greased and floured 8-inch pans at 350° for 30 to 35 minutes.

FROSTING:
1 box powdered sugar, sifted
5½ teaspoons margarine
4 tablespoons hot coffee
2 tablespoons cocoa
1½ teaspoons vanilla

Mix ingredients together and beat on high speed until well blended. You may double recipe for ample frosting.

Joyce Beasley
Lufkin, Texas

TEXAS SHEET CAKE

2 cups flour
2 cups sugar
½ teaspoon salt
2 sticks butter
1 cup water
4 tablespoons cocoa
½ cup sour cream
2 eggs
1 teaspoon soda
1 teaspoon vanilla

"I have had this recipe for approximately twenty years and did not just now tack 'Texas' on it. It came to me that way because of the large quantity it makes."

Put flour, sugar and salt in large bowl. In small heavy pan bring butter, water and cocoa to a boil. Take from heat and add immediately to dry ingredients. Add sour cream, eggs, soda and vanilla. Mix until blended. Pour into lightly greased and floured 10½ × 15½-inch pan. Bake for 20 to 25 minutes at 375°. Frost with Cocoa Butter Frosting.

COCOA BUTTER FROSTING:
6 tablespoons milk
4 tablespoons cocoa
1 stick butter
1 cup nuts
1 box powdered sugar
1 teaspoon vanilla

Boil milk, cocoa, and butter until bubbly. Mix in nuts, sugar and vanilla. Beat until smooth and spread over warm cake.

Barbara J. Wetter
Houston, Texas

RUM CAKE

1 cup chopped pecans or walnuts
1 box yellow cake mix
1 small box vanilla instant pudding
4 eggs
½ cup vegetable oil
½ cup dark rum
½ cup water

Preheat oven to 325°. Grease and flour a 10-inch tube or bundt pan. Sprinkle nuts in bottom of pan. Mix all cake ingredients together. Pour batter over nuts. Bake 1 hour. Cool. Invert on serving plate. Prick holes in top of cake. Spoon and brush glaze evenly over top and sides. Allow cake to absorb glaze.

"This is a goodie!"

GLAZE:
1 stick butter
¼ cup water
1 cup sugar
½ cup rum (80 proof)

Melt butter in saucepan. Stir in water and sugar. Boil for 5 minutes, stirring constantly. Remove from heat. Stir in rum.

Helen Anders
La Marque, Texas

ITALIAN CREAM CAKE

1 teaspoon soda
1 cup buttermilk
2 cups sugar
1 stick margarine
½ cup shortening
5 eggs, separated
2 cups sifted all-purpose flour
1 teaspoon vanilla extract
1 cup chopped pecans
1 4-ounce can flaked coconut

Preheat oven to 325°. Combine soda and buttermilk, and let stand a few minutes. Cream sugar, margarine and shortening. Add egg yolks, 1 at a time, beating well after each addition. Add buttermilk alternately with flour to creamed mixture. Stir in vanilla. Beat egg whites until stiff. Fold in egg whites, then gently stir in pecans and coconut. Bake in 3 greased and floured 9-inch layer pans for 25 minutes or until cake tests done. Frost cooled cake with Cream-Cheese Icing.

CREAM-CHEESE ICING:

1 8-ounce package cream cheese, softened
1 stick margarine, at room temperature
1 teaspoon vanilla
1 pound powdered sugar

Beat cream cheese and margarine well; add vanilla. Beat in sugar a little at a time until desired spreading consistency.

Lorena Pizzitola
Houston, Texas

FAVORITE SPICE CAKE

1 cup brown sugar
½ cup shortening
2 cups cake flour
½ teaspoon salt
1 teaspoon baking powder
½ teaspoon soda
1 teaspoon cinnamon
½ teaspoon nutmeg
½ teaspoon allspice
¾ cup buttermilk
2 eggs

Cream the sugar and shortening. Sift all the dry ingredients and add alternately with the buttermilk. Then add the whole eggs and mix thoroughly. Grease and flour 3 cake pans and divide the batter evenly. Bake at 350° for approximately 30 minutes or until the layers turn loose from the edges of the pans. Ice with Powdered-Sugar Icing.

POWDERED-SUGAR ICING:

1 stick butter, at room temperature
½ cup shortening
1 box powdered sugar
3 egg whites
1 teaspoon vanilla
¼ teaspoon salt
Chopped nuts

Combine the butter and shortening. Add the sugar a little at a time and then add 1 egg white at a time, beating well after each addition. When the mixture is smooth and fluffy, add the vanilla and salt. Ice the cake and sprinkle nuts over the layers and on top.

Jean King Sitterle
Houston, Texas

LEMON CHIFFON CAKE

2½ cups cake flour
1½ cups sugar
3 teaspoons baking powder
1 teaspoon salt
½ cup vegetable oil
5 egg yolks
¾ cup water
1 teaspoon vanilla
2 teaspoons finely grated lemon peel
1 cup (8) egg whites
½ teaspoon cream of tartar

Sift dry ingredients in bowl. Add vegetable oil, egg yolks, water, vanilla and lemon peel. Mix well. Combine egg whites and cream of tartar. Beat to very stiff peaks. Pour egg yolk batter over the egg whites and fold in. Bake in prepared tube pan at 350° for about 1 hour.

Frost with a lemon-flavored powdered-sugar icing that has been tinted with yellow food coloring.

Cleddie H. Harvey
Palacios, Texas

PIES

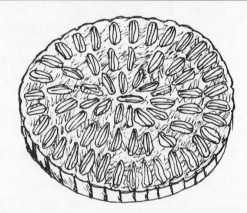

BETTER-THAN-PECAN PIE

1 stick margarine
1 cup sugar
2 eggs, beaten
½ cup flaked coconut
½ cup raisins
½ cup chopped pecans
1 teaspoon vanilla
1 teaspoon vinegar

Melt margarine; add sugar, eggs, coconut, raisins and pecans; and mix well. Add vanilla and vinegar. Pour into an 8- or 9-inch unbaked piecrust. Bake at 325° for about 35 to 40 minutes or until set in the middle.

Caroline Blaylock
Austin, Texas

BASIC PIECRUST

½ cup margarine or shortening
1¼ cups flour
2 tablespoons cold water

Cut margarine or shortening into flour with a fork or wire piecrust-cutter. Add water gradually to form a slightly sticky ball. Roll out on floured board and press into pie pan. Bake piecrust in a 350° oven for 15 minutes. This crust is for fruit fillings, custards, etc. Leave unbaked for pecan filling. Double recipe for 2-crust pies.

ALLIE MAE'S PECAN PIE

1 cup sugar
1 tablespoon flour
1 cup light corn syrup
3 eggs
Pinch of salt
1 teaspoon vanilla
1 cup whole pecans

"There are probably fifty different recipes for pecan pie, but this particular pie has a richness which sets it apart from all the others."

Beat well the sugar, flour, corn syrup, eggs, salt and vanilla. Add pecans. Bake in unbaked pie shell at 300° for 50 minutes.

Anne Thorpe
Houston, Texas

TEXAS PECAN PIE

⅓ cup butter or margarine, melted
1 cup sugar
1 cup light corn syrup
½ teaspoon salt
2 teaspoons vanilla extract
4 eggs
1 cup coarsely chopped pecans
1 unbaked 9-inch pastry shell

Combine butter, sugar, corn syrup, salt and vanilla in a medium mixing bowl; beat well. Add eggs and beat well. Stir in pecans. Pour into pastry shell. Bake at 375° for 45 to 50 minutes.

Flora Bowie
Splendora, Texas

PECAN-PRALINE PIE

First, make the meringue shell:

3 egg whites
1 cup sugar
1 cup crushed Pecan Sandies cookies
¼ cup chopped pecans

Beat egg whites until stiff. Slowly beat in sugar, and then fold in cookie crumbs and pecans. Butter a glass pie plate and turn mixture into plate, building up rim of shell. Bake in 325° oven for 30 minutes; then turn off oven and allow shell to cool in oven.
   Now, make the filling:

1 quart pecan-praline-flavored ice cream
Bottled caramel topping
¼ cup chopped pecans

Spoon the ice cream into the cooled shell; drizzle with caramel topping and pecans. Cover with plastic wrap, and freeze. Remove from freezer 5 minutes before serving.

Nancy Kay Ramsey
Elgin, Texas

BUTTER-RUM PECAN PIE

2 or more cups broken pecans
3 9-inch unbaked pie shells
6 eggs
1 cup light brown sugar
2 cups light corn syrup
⅔ cup soft butter
2 teaspoons vanilla
¾ cup dark rum
Pinch of salt

Sprinkle pecans on bottom of pie shell. (If using frozen shells, coat well with soft butter first.) Combine all ingredients and pour over pecans. Bake at 325° for 35 to 40 minutes. Don't overbake, as the center of the filling will set as it cools. Chill and cover with whipped cream, Cool Whip or French vanilla ice cream.

Helen Hill
Spicewood, Texas

MYSTERY PECAN PIE

1 8-ounce package cream cheese
1/3 cup sugar
1/4 teaspoon salt
1 teaspoon vanilla
4 eggs
1 unbaked pie shell
1 1/4 cups pecans
1/4 cup sugar
1 cup light or dark corn syrup
1 teaspoon vanilla

Combine cream cheese, 1/3 cup sugar, salt, vanilla and 1 of the eggs. Beat well and spread in bottom of pie shell. Sprinkle pecans over cheese layer. Combine 3 eggs, 1/4 cup sugar, corn syrup and vanilla, and pour over pecans. Bake at 375° for 40 minutes.

Fern P. Harvey
Palacios, Texas

PECAN DELIGHT

3 egg whites
1 cup sugar
1 cup graham-cracker crumbs
1 teaspoon vanilla
1 cup chopped nuts
Whipped cream

Beat egg whites until stiff. Beat in sugar. Fold in cracker crumbs, vanilla and nuts. Place in well-greased 9-inch pie pan. Bake at 350° for 20 minutes. Chill. Top with whipped cream.

Cindy Stubblefield
Stafford, Texas

MOMMA'S GERMAN APPLE PIE

EGG YOLK PASTRY:
5 cups flour
4 teaspoons sugar
1/2 teaspoon baking powder
1/2 teaspoon salt
1 1/2 cups lard or shortening
2 egg yolks
Cold water

Combine dry ingredients, and cut in lard or shortening. Place egg yolks in measuring cup and stir until smooth. Blend in enough water to make a scant cupful. Sprinkle gradually over dry ingredients to make soft dough. Divide dough in half. Roll out and line bottom of one 11 × 17-inch jelly-roll pan. Roll out remaining dough and set aside. Prepare filling.

APPLE PIE FILLING:
5 pounds tart apples, pared, cored and sliced
4 teaspoons lemon juice
¾ cup sugar
¾ cup brown sugar, packed
1 teaspoon cinnamon
¼ teaspoon salt
¼ teaspoon nutmeg

Put apples into large bowl. Sprinkle lemon juice over apples. Combine remaining ingredients and mix into apples. Spread evenly over pastry. Top with remaining pastry and seal, crimping edges. Brush with milk and sprinkle with sugar. Cut vents in top. Bake at 400° for 50 minutes. When pie is cool, drizzle with frosting.

FROSTING:
1 cup powdered sugar
2 tablespoons milk

Mix until smooth. To serve, cut pie into squares. Yields 24 squares.

Amelia F. Mettke
Austin, Texas

MOTHER MAC'S APPLE PIE

3 cups sliced apples
¾ cup sugar
1 cup sour cream
2 tablespoons flour
1 egg, well beaten
1 teaspoon vanilla
Pinch of salt
1 unbaked pie shell

Mix filling ingredients and pour into pie shell. Add topping and bake at 350° for 45 to 60 minutes.

TOPPING:
⅓ cup flour
⅓ cup sugar
¼ cup butter, softened
1 teaspoon cinnamon

Mix ingredients to crumbly texture and sprinkle on top of pie.

Jeanie Ingle
Manvel, Texas

BERRY PIE

2 to 3 cups berries
1 10-inch unbaked pie shell
2 eggs, beaten
½ cup sour cream
1½ cups sugar
⅓ cup flour

Sprinkle berries on pie shell. Combine remaining ingredients and pour over berries. Put crumb topping over pie and bake at 350° for about 45 minutes.

CRUMB TOPPING:
½ cup flour
½ cup sugar
¼ cup butter

Mix well and sprinkle over pie.

Doris Doskocil
Crosby, Texas

FRESH PEACH PIE

7 fresh peaches, peeled and pitted
½ cup water
3 tablespoons cornstarch
1 cup sugar
1 baked pie shell
Whipped cream

Mash 3 of the peaches and cook with water, cornstarch and sugar until thick and clear. Cool. Slice remaining peaches and place in baked pie shell. Pour cooked mixture over sliced peaches. Top with whipped cream. Cool in refrigerator at least 3 hours before serving.

Annie R. Majnik
Cleveland, Texas

RED BONNET RAISIN PIE

2 eggs, lightly beaten
¾ cup sugar
Dash of salt
½ teaspoon cinnamon
¼ teaspoon nutmeg
¼ teaspoon ground cloves
1 cup sour cream
1 cup raisins
1 unbaked 8-inch pie shell

Combine eggs, sugar, salt and spices. Mix well. Stir in sour cream and raisins. Pour into pie shell. Bake at 425° for 10 minutes. Reduce heat to 350° and bake an additional 30 minutes, or until knife inserted near center comes out clean.

Fureen Lerch
Baytown, Texas

SLICED-ORANGE PIE

4 medium oranges
1 9-inch unbaked pie shell
1 egg, beaten
¾ cup sugar
⅓ cup flour
½ cup water
½ teaspoon salt
Grated rind of 1 orange
2 tablespoons butter

"This is unusual, but good. It is my original and I am eighty-five years old."

Peel whole oranges, removing white parts. Slice thinly. Discard seeds. Spread sliced oranges over bottom of pie shell. Mix well the egg, sugar, flour, water, salt and grated rind, and pour over oranges. Dot with butter. Start in a preheated oven at 400°. After 10 minutes, reduce heat to 350° and bake 45 minutes longer.

A lattice crust may be put on top, but it is not necessary.

Mrs. William Foss
La Grange, Texas

PLUM PIE

4 to 5 cups pitted fresh purple plums, halved
1¼ cups sugar
2 tablespoons flour
2 tablespoons lemon juice
⅛ teaspoon salt
Pastry for double-crust pie
1 tablespoon butter

Combine plums, sugar, flour, lemon juice and salt. Line pie pan with pastry, add filling, dot with butter, and cover with top crust. Sprinkle with milk and a bit of sugar to make crust brown and sparkly. Bake at 450° for 10 minutes; reduce temperature to 350° and bake 35 minutes longer, or until plums are tender. The plums turn a beautiful red after baking.

Judy McCleary
Houston, Texas

BUTTERMILK PIE I

1½ cups sugar
2 cups buttermilk
3 tablespoons flour or cornstarch
3 egg yolks
2 tablespoons lemon extract
1 tablespoon butter
1 baked pie shell

Mix ingredients together and cook in heavy pot, stirring constantly. Cook until thick. Pour into baked pie shell.

MERINGUE:
3 egg whites
9 tablespoons sugar

Beat egg whites until stiff, then gradually add sugar. Cover pie with meringue and brown lightly at 350° for several minutes.

"I am sixty-nine years old, and my mother was making these pies years before I was born—and cooking them on a wood stove, at that."

Claire R. Curbello
Sweeny, Texas

BUTTERMILK PIE II

3 eggs
1¾ cups sugar
1 teaspoon vanilla
1 rounded tablespoon flour
¾ stick butter, melted
½ cup buttermilk
1 unbaked pie shell

Mix eggs, sugar, vanilla and flour. Add melted butter and buttermilk. Mix well. Pour into pie shell and bake at 350° about 50 minutes or until middle doesn't shake.

Jackie McIntosh
Fort Worth, Texas

GRAPEFRUIT CHIFFON PIE

1 tablespoon unflavored gelatin
¼ cup cold water
4 eggs
½ cup grapefruit juice
1 tablespoon lemon juice
1 grapefruit, sectioned
1 cup sugar
1 baked pie shell

Soften gelatin in cold water. Separate eggs. Beat egg yolks slightly. Combine gelatin and egg yolks with all other filling ingredients except egg whites. Cook in double boiler, stirring constantly until slightly thick (about 5 minutes). Remove from heat. Beat egg whites until stiff, but not dry. Fold egg whites into the hot mixture and mix thoroughly. Let cool. Pour into baked pie shell. Chill.

Adela Haedge
Bellville, Texas

COCONUT PIE

1¼ cups sugar
3 tablespoons flour
½ teaspoon salt
4 eggs, separated
2¼ cups milk
1 cup coconut
1 teaspoon vanilla
2 tablespoons margarine
1 baked pie shell
Meringue
Additional coconut

Sift sugar, flour and salt together. Beat egg yolks in milk and add dry mixture. Pour mixture in double boiler. Add coconut, vanilla and margarine. Cook until thick. Pour in baked pie shell.

MERINGUE:
4 egg whites
4 tablespoons sugar
1 tablespoon vanilla

Beat egg whites until stiff, then gradually add sugar and vanilla. Put meringue on pie and sprinkle with coconut. Bake 10 to 12 minutes at 375°. Cool and refrigerate.

Opal Hayley
La Marque, Texas

EGG CUSTARD PIE

3 large eggs
½ teaspoon salt
¼ teaspoon nutmeg
½ cup sugar
2¼ cups milk
1 unbaked pie shell

Beat eggs well. Add salt, nutmeg, sugar and milk. Mix well. Pour into unbaked pie shell and bake for about 1 hour at 300° or until firm in the middle. Let cool.

Anne Lytle
Dayton, Texas

JEFF DAVIS PIE

2 cups sugar
½ cup butter
1 tablespoon flour
½ teaspoon salt
1 teaspoon vanilla
4 eggs
1 cup milk
1 unbaked pie shell

Combine sugar and butter in bowl, creaming until smooth. Blend in flour, salt and vanilla. Beat eggs slightly, and add to creamed mixture. Add milk, slowly stirring until mixture is smooth. Pour mixture into pie shell. Bake at 275° for 1 hour or until firm and golden brown. Serve slightly warm.

Theresa Younger
Dayton, Texas

COPE'S PIE

4 eggs
2 cups sugar
2 tablespoons cornmeal
1 tablespoon flour
¼ cup lemon juice
¼ cup butter
¼ cup sweet milk
1 unbaked pie shell

Mix filling ingredients. Pour into unbaked pie shell. Bake at 350° for about 40 minutes.
    Variation: Add ½ cup coconut to filling.

Dana C. Rogers
Lufkin, Texas

VINEGAR PIE

2 tablespoons butter
½ cup sugar
3 tablespoons flour
⅛ teaspoon salt
1 egg, separated
2 tablespoons vinegar
2 teaspoons lemon juice
1 cup water
1 9-inch unbaked pie shell

Cream butter and sugar. Add dry ingredients and blend well. Add beaten egg yolk. Add vinegar, lemon juice and water. Cook in top of double boiler until thickened, stirring constantly. Beat egg white. Fold beaten egg white into mixture. Bake pie shell for 5 minutes at 350°. Pour filling into shell and return to oven to continue baking until crust is brown (about 40 minutes).

Variation: ½ teaspoon cinnamon, ¼ teaspoon cloves and ¼ teaspoon allspice may be added to the filling before pouring into pastry shell.

Edith Mandala
Houston, Texas

SWEET POTATO PIE

1⅓ cups sugar
½ cup butter or margarine
⅓ cup half-and-half
3 eggs
1 cup mashed cooked sweet potatoes
½ teaspoon nutmeg
½ teaspoon cinnamon
¼ teaspoon salt
1 teaspoon vanilla
1 unbaked 9-inch pie shell

Preheat oven to 350°. Cream sugar and butter in mixing bowl until light and fluffy. Add half-and-half, and blend well with mixer. Add eggs, 1 at a time, beating well after each addition. Add sweet potatoes, nutmeg, cinnamon, salt and vanilla, and blend well. Pour into pie shell. Bake 50 minutes, or until knife inserted 1 inch from edge comes out clean. Cool before serving.

Bobbie Barrow
Hankamer, Texas

OLD-FASHIONED CHESS PIE

1½ cups sugar
2 tablespoons cornmeal
½ cup butter
1 tablespoon vinegar
1 teaspoon vanilla
4 eggs, beaten
1 unbaked pie shell

Combine first 5 ingredients. Stir in eggs and mix well. Pour into pie shell and bake 50 to 55 minutes at 350°. Pie has the flavor of lemon.

Mrs. Wes Cargal
Nacogdoches, Texas

CHEESE PIE

1 pound cottage cheese
¼ cup milk
⅓ cup sugar
½ cup chopped raisins
3 eggs, beaten
2 tablespoons melted shortening
Juice of 1 lemon
Grated rind of 1 lemon
1 baked pie shell

Put cottage cheese through sieve and add other filling ingredients. Mix well and pour into cooled pie shell. Bake at 350° until firm in center, about 15 to 20 minutes.

Jane Luttrell
Pasadena, Texas

IRISH POTATO PIE

1¼ cups sugar
2½ tablespoons flour
3 eggs, well beaten
¾ cup potatoes, mashed
3 tablespoons margarine, melted
2 teaspoons lemon flavoring
1½ cups milk
1 9-inch unbaked pie crust

Sift sugar and flour together and set aside. Beat eggs and mashed potatoes together, then add sugar and flour mixture, margarine, lemon flavoring and milk. Pour into unbaked pie crust and bake at 350° until set and inserted knife comes out clean. You might need to cover top of crust with foil to keep it from burning. The pie will be slightly brown on top.

Vada Hyman
Liberty Hill, Texas

FRENCH SILK PIE

1 stick butter or margarine
¾ cup sugar
1 teaspoon vanilla
2 squares unsweetened chocolate, melted
3 eggs
1 baked pastry shell
Sweetened whipped cream flavored with vanilla or rum

Cream well the butter, sugar and vanilla. Stir in the melted chocolate, and add eggs 1 at a time, beating 2 minutes after each. Pour filling into pie shell and refrigerate overnight or several hours. Serve with sweetened whipped cream.

Mable Bacon
Houston, Texas

"I have had this recipe since 1956, and it is unusual and very delicious."

CHOCOLATE CREAM PIE

¼ cup flour
1¼ cups sugar
⅛ teaspoon salt
4 tablespoons cocoa
1⅓ cups milk
1 small can evaporated milk
3 egg yolks, beaten
½ teaspoon vanilla
2 tablespoons margarine
1 baked pastry shell, dusted with powdered sugar
Meringue

"My husband made ten or twelve pies before settling on this recipe."
—*Mrs. Hoytt Jones*

Combine flour, sugar, salt and cocoa, add milks, and cook over low heat until thick, stirring constantly. Stir small amount of hot mixture into egg yolks, pour back into saucepan, and cook until thick. Add vanilla and margarine. Pour into baked pastry shell that has been sprinkled with powdered sugar. Top with meringue. Bake at 350° for 10 minutes.

Hoytt Jones
Odessa, Texas

OLD-FASHIONED CHOCOLATE PIE

1½ cups sugar
½ cup flour
¼ teaspoon salt
6 tablespoons cocoa
2 cups milk
3 egg yolks
1½ teaspoons vanilla
1 tablespoon butter
1 baked pie shell

Mix all the dry ingredients. Scald milk in top of double boiler. Add all dry ingredients, stirring until mixture thickens. Add egg yolks; cook until thick. Add butter and vanilla. Pour in a baked pie shell and heap meringue on top. Brown under broiler.

MERINGUE:
3 egg whites
⅛ teaspoon salt
6 tablespoons sugar

Beat egg whites with salt until stiff. Add sugar gradually, beating after each tablespoon.

Allene Eberle
Porter, Texas

CHOCOLATE CREAM-CHEESE PIE

2 cups flour
1½ sticks margarine, softened slightly
1 cup chopped nuts
2 8-ounce packages cream cheese
1½ cups powdered sugar
2 cups Cool Whip or sweetened whipped cream
2 large packages chocolate instant pudding mix
3 cups milk
Additional Cool Whip or sweetened whipped cream

Make a crust by mixing flour, margarine and nuts, and pressing mixture into a 9 × 13-inch pan. Bake at 350° for 2 minutes. Let cool.

Combine cream cheese, powdered sugar and Cool Whip, and spread over crust.

Beat chocolate-pudding mix and milk until mixture begins to thicken. Pour over the cream-cheese layer. Top with additional Cool Whip.

Yvonnie Roane
Houston, Texas

MAE MURRELL'S JACK DANIELS PIE

CRUST:
½ cup flour
⅛ teaspoon baking powder
⅛ teaspoon salt
½ cup soft butter
1 cup sugar
2 eggs, beaten until light and fluffy
2 ounces unsweetened chocolate
½ teaspoon vanilla
1 cup chopped nuts

Sift flour, baking powder and salt. Set aside. Mix butter, sugar and beaten eggs in small bowl on medium speed of mixer. Add melted chocolate and vanilla. Add sifted mixture and fold in nuts. Pour into lightly floured 9 × 13-inch baking pan, and bake 20 minutes at 325°.

FILLING:
3 eggs
1½ cups sugar
⅓ cup plus 2 tablespoons flour
¼ teaspoon salt
3 cups scalded milk
3 tablespoons butter
3 to 4 tablespoons Jack Daniels Black Label whiskey
Sweetened whipped cream
Grated German's sweet chocolate

Beat eggs until fluffy. Add sugar mixed with flour and salt. Stir in milk. Cook in double boiler until mixture thickens. Add butter. Remove from heat and add Jack Daniels. Cool. Pour into cooled crust. Top with sweetened whipped cream and then grated chocolate. Chill several hours before serving.

Mae Murrell

MAGGIE MAHLER'S ICEBOX PIE

1 package gelatin
½ cup cold water
1½ cups milk
¾ cup sugar
2 teaspoons vanilla
½ pint whipping cream
Vanilla wafers
⅓ cup pecan halves

Dissolve gelatin in water. Stir sugar into milk and then scald mixture. Combine gelatin and milk mixtures; cool.

Add vanilla. Put in refrigerator. When mixture begins to congeal, whip cream. Fold cream into mixture, stirring until well mixed.

Put in a plastic bag enough vanilla wafers to line a 9-inch square glass baking dish, and crush until fine. Line dish with crushed cookies. Pour cream mixture on top of cookies. Place pecan halves on top of cream mixture. Return to refrigerator to jell. Cut in squares and serve.

Pat Mitchell McNabb
Midland, Texas

HONEYSUCKLE PIE

½ cup sugar
1 tablespoon lemon juice
1 cup coconut
1 8-ounce package cream cheese, softened
1 baked 9-inch pastry or graham-cracker pie shell
1¼ cups apricot preserves
1 package vanilla pudding mix, cooked according to package directions and cooled
Nutmeg
Cool Whip or sweetened whipped cream

"This pie keeps well, but usually none is left because it is so delicious."

Blend sugar, lemon juice and coconut into cream cheese. Spread evenly over bottom of pie shell.

Spoon apricot preserves into pudding. Spread evenly over cream-cheese mixture. Sprinkle with freshly grated nutmeg. Cover completely with Cool Whip. If you like nutmeg, add some to top of Cool Whip. Refrigerate until ready to serve.

Lou Nell Sowell
Huntsville, Texas

PEACH COBBLER

CRUST:
1⅓ cups flour
½ cup plus 1 tablespoon butter-flavored shortening
½ teaspoon salt
3 tablespoons cold water

Mix flour, salt and shortening in large mixing bowl. Mix until all is evenly blended. Add water and stir with spoon. Roll out on floured board. Roll out large enough to lap back over for top crust.

FILLING:
3 cups fresh or canned peaches
2 heaping tablespoons tapioca
½ teaspoon salt
1 cup sugar
1 tablespoon lemon juice
¼ teaspoon almond extract
Butter
Sugar and cinnamon

Stir together all ingredients except butter and sugar-and-cinnamon mixture. Pour into crust and dot with butter. Fold over crust to center, sprinkle with sugar and cinnamon. Bake at 350° until golden brown.

Janet Hronek
Somerville, Texas

GLO'S PEACH COBBLER

1 cup sugar
½ cup butter
2 cups flour
4 teaspoons baking powder
½ teaspoon salt
1 cup milk
10 to 12 fresh peaches, peeled and chopped
1½ cups sugar
Juice of ½ lemon
1 teaspoon almond flavoring

Beat 1 cup sugar and butter together. Add sifted dry ingredients, then add milk. Beat well and pour into buttered 9 × 13-inch pan. Mix chopped peaches, 1½ cups sugar, lemon juice and almond flavoring. Cook in microwave on full power for 5 minutes, stirring once. Using a large spoon, gently spread peaches and juices on top of batter and bake at 325° for 45 to 60 minutes. Good with whipped cream or vanilla ice cream.

Gloria R. Payette
San Leon, Texas

ASSORTED DESSERTS

MY MAMA'S EGG CUSTARD

4 eggs, well beaten
Pinch of salt
1 cup sugar
3 cups milk
2 teaspoons vanilla
1 tablespoon melted butter

Butter a casserole. Mix all ingredients. Bake in custard cups set in a pan of water at 350° about 45 minutes or until a knife inserted near center comes out clean.

Alice K. Williams
Austin, Texas

LEMON CAKE PUDDING

2 eggs, separated
¼ teaspoon salt
½ cup sugar
1 tablespoon grated lemon rind
5 tablespoons lemon juice
2 tablespoons butter, melted
¼ cup sugar
3 tablespoons flour
1 cup milk

"Serves four—unless my husband Warren is there."

Heat oven to 350°. Grease a 1-quart casserole. Beat egg whites with salt until moist peaks form. Gradually add ½ cup sugar, beating until stiff. Beat yolks with lemon rind, juice and melted butter. Stir in ¼ cup sugar, mixed with flour, and add milk. Fold into beaten egg whites. Pour batter into casserole. Set in pan containing ½ inch hot water. Bake uncovered 30 to 45 minutes or until top is firm and brown.

Melanie Thompson
Austin, Texas

CAKE-TOP PUDDING

⅔ cup sugar
3 tablespoons butter
4 eggs
⅓ cup lemon juice
2 teaspoons lemon rind
¼ teaspoon salt
3 tablespoons flour
1 cup milk
4 egg whites, stiffly beaten

Cream sugar and butter; add eggs. Mix well and add lemon juice, rind, salt and flour. Beat well. Stir in milk. Fold in egg whites. Pour into baking dish. Set in pan of hot water. Bake in 325° oven for 40 minutes or until lightly brown, or bake in 6 individual baking dishes. Serves 6.

Lenee MacDonald
Romayor, Texas

BANANA PUDDING

2 cups sugar
Pinch of salt
⅔ cup cornstarch
4 cups milk
6 egg yolks, beaten
2 teaspoons vanilla
2 tablespoons butter
1 large box vanilla wafers
6 large ripe bananas

"The people in my community are crazy about this pudding."

Put first 5 ingredients in top of double boiler, and cook, stirring constantly, until thick. Take off burner and add vanilla and butter.

Layer vanilla wafers, in a 9 × 13-inch ovenproof dish, then sliced bananas, then half of filling. Repeat layers. Put meringue on top of pudding and bake at 425° until brown. Serves about 20.

MERINGUE:
6 egg whites
12 tablespoons sugar

Beat egg whites until stiff, then add sugar a little at a time, continuing to beat.

Della Graham
Austin, Texas

BREAD PUDDING

2 cups bread crumbs soaked in 2 cups milk
½ cup sugar
4 eggs, beaten
1 teaspoon vanilla
Pinch of salt
½ stick of melted margarine

To soaked bread crumbs add remaining ingredients and mix well. Bake in a 1½-quart dish for 45 minutes at 350°. Serve warm with sauce.

SAUCE:
½ stick margarine
¼ cup flour
Pinch of salt
2 cups milk
¾ cup sugar
1 teaspoon vanilla

Melt margarine in a pan. Add flour and salt. Stir until smooth. Add milk and sugar. Stir until thick and smooth. Add vanilla.

Bobbie Dykes
Bay City, Texas

FRENCH BREAD PUDDING

½ cup chopped pecans
½ cup softened margarine
1 cup sugar
4 eggs
1¾ cups milk
1½ teaspoons cinnamon
1½ teaspoons nutmeg
1½ teaspoons vanilla
5 cups French bread cubes
⅓ cup raisins

Spread pecans on baking sheet and toast 8 minutes at 350°. Set aside. Cream margarine; gradually add sugar, beating well. Add eggs and beat well. Stir in milk, spices and vanilla. Mix well. Stir in pecans, bread and raisins, stirring well, but just until bread is moistened. Spoon into greased 8 × 8-inch pan. Let stand 15 minutes. Cover and bake 45 minutes at 350°, then uncovered 10 minutes longer. Serve warm.

Shirley Wylie
Livingston, Texas

GERMAN SWEET RICE

½ cup raw rice (not instant)
⅓ cup water
2 cups milk
1 tablespoon butter
Salt
½ cup sugar
Cinnamon

Cook rice in water, milk, butter and salt until done. Add sugar just before rice is done. Stir constantly during cooking. Sprinkle with small amount of sugar and cinnamon to serve family style.

LaVerna Stolz
Brenham, Texas

GLORIFIED RICE

1 cup uncooked rice
3 cups milk
½ cup sugar
½ teaspoon salt
2 eggs, beaten
1 cup whipping cream
2 tablespoons powdered sugar
1 teaspoon vanilla
½ teaspoon extract
1 16-ounce can fruit cocktail, well drained

Cook rice in milk in top of double boiler until tender, stirring occasionally, about 1 hour. Add sugar and salt. Add a little hot mixture gradually to beaten eggs. Stir into remaining hot mixture. Blend well, cool. Whip cream with powdered sugar, vanilla and almond extract. Fold into cool rice. Fold in fruit cocktail. Chill.

Margaret Zacharias
Alvin, Texas

STRAWBERRY MOUSSE

2 egg whites
Pinch of salt
½ cup sugar
¼ pound fresh strawberries (about 6 large berries)
1 cup whipped cream

In bowl, beat egg whites with salt until they hold soft peaks. Beat in sugar, a little at a time. Continue to beat the meringue until it is stiff and shiny. Puree strawberries and fold into meringue. Fold in whipped cream. Divide mixture among 6 small dishes or stemmed glasses. Chill at least 3 hours.

Mrs. J. P. Pfieffer
Bastrop, Texas

PEPPERMINT ICE CREAM

For 1-gallon freezer:

1 pound peppermint sticks, crushed and soaked in 1 pint of
    whipping cream overnight
1 can sweetened condensed milk
Milk

Mix peppermint sticks, whipping cream and sweetened condensed milk and pour into freezer. Finish filling freezer container to recommended capacity, with milk. Freeze, remove dasher and repack.

Mrs. Fred McIntosh
Houston, Texas

CHOCOLATE ICE CREAM

10 eggs, beaten
2½ cups sugar
1 can chocolate syrup
1 pint whipping cream, whipped
⅓ tablespoon salt
1 tablespoon vanilla

Beat eggs, then add sugar; add syrup, whipped cream, salt and vanilla. Put mixture into freezer and finish filling can to recommended capacity, with milk. Makes 1½ gallons.

Arlette Williams
Edna, Texas

PEANUT BUTTER FUDGE

2 cups sugar
2 tablespoons cocoa
⅓ cup light corn syrup
½ cup milk
2 heaping tablespoons peanut butter
1 tablespoon butter
1 teaspoon vanilla

Combine first 4 ingredients in saucepan and bring to a soft-ball stage or 225°. Take off stove and add peanut butter, butter and vanilla. Do not stir. Let cool for 15 minutes, then stir and stir until dipping stage. Spoon onto wax paper with 2 teaspoons.

Mary Parker
Pasadena, Texas

PEANUT CANDY

½ cup peanut butter
1 cup chocolate bits
1 cup salted peanuts

Heat peanut butter and chocolate bits in top of double boiler until melted. Then stir in peanuts and drop by teaspoonfuls on wax paper in clusters. Makes about 20 pieces.

Yvonne Whitton Kingsley
Arcadia, Texas

PEANUT BUTTER– CHOCOLATE FUDGE

1 12-ounce package peanut butter chips
1 14-ounce can sweetened condensed milk
¼ cup butter or margarine
½ cup chopped peanuts
1 6-ounce package semisweet chocolate morsels

In large saucepan, melt peanut butter chips, 1 cup sweetened condensed milk and 2 tablespoons butter. Stir occasionally. Remove from heat and stir in peanuts. Spread mixture in a wax-paper-lined 8-inch square pan.

In small saucepan, melt chocolate morsels, remaining sweetened condensed milk and butter (mixture should be creamy). Spread chocolate mixture on top of peanut butter mixture. Chill 2 hours or until firm.

Turn out onto cutting board; peel off wax paper and cut fudge into squares.

Frieda Wolf
La Porte, Texas

MISSISSIPPI MUD CANDY

1 stick butter
1 12-ounce package chocolate chips
1 12-ounce package butterscotch chips
1 10½-ounce package miniature marshmallows
1 cup chopped pecans

In microwave, melt butter and then add chips. Stir and melt mixture, but do not cook. Mix marshmallows and pecans into chocolate mixture. Pour into greased shallow baking pan. Cut in small squares after cooling in refrigerator.

Elizabeth B. Heishman
San Antonio, Texas

GRANDMOTHER'S WALNUT DIVINITY

2½ cups sugar
1 cup water
¾ cup white corn syrup
5 egg whites
Pinch of salt
2 teaspoons vanilla
½ teaspoon almond extract
15 drops lemon juice
1 cup chopped walnuts
5 drops red food coloring

Cook sugar, water and corn syrup to firm-ball stage (250°). Beat egg whites with salt. Pour syrup over egg whites. Add extracts, lemon juice, walnuts and food coloring. Beat until mixture is thick and holds shape. Drop on foil. Makes 100 pieces.

Fern P. Harvey
Palacios, Texas

COCOA PUFFS

1 cup sugar
½ cup light corn syrup
¼ cup honey
1 cup crunchy peanut butter
6 cups Cocoa Puffs

Boil sugar, syrup and honey for about 3 minutes. Turn off burner. Add peanut butter. Pour mixture over Cocoa Puffs and dip by teaspoon onto wax paper.

Era Berrier
Pasadena, Texas

BRANDY TOFFEE

1 pound margarine
2 cups sugar
2 tablespoons brandy
¾ cup walnuts
2 tablespoons white corn syrup
1 cup almonds
1 8-ounce package sweet chocolate

Mix together all ingredients except almonds and chocolate. Cook to 298°. Add nuts. Pour in pan. Cool. Melt chocolate and spread over candy while it is hot. Break into pieces when cold.

Fern P. Harvey
Palacios, Texas

FROSTED SPICE PECANS

1 egg white, beaten slightly with fork
2 tablespoons water
½ cup sugar
½ teaspoon salt
¼ teaspoon cinnamon
¼ teaspoon cloves
¼ teaspoon allspice
2 cups pecan halves

Combine egg whites, water and sugar. Blend salt and spices, and add to sugar mixture. Add pecans. Stir until each nut is well coated. Spread on a greased cookie sheet. Bake at 250° for 1 hour.

Wilda Deas
Houston, Texas

SUGAR-AND-SPICE NUTS

1 egg white
2 cups pecans or walnuts
¼ cup brown sugar
1 teaspoon cinnamon

Beat egg white with a fork and combine with nuts in a bowl, mixing well. Combine brown sugar and cinnamon, then add to nut mixture, blending thoroughly. Place mixture in a 9-inch glass pie plate, and cook at high power of microwave, stirring occasionally, for about 4 minutes or until coating loses its gloss.

Dorothy Ann Rothermel
Brenham, Texas

FIESTA PRALINES

1 cup sugar
½ cup brown sugar
¼ cup milk
1 cup pecans
1 tablespoon butter
1 teaspoon vanilla

Mix in heavy skillet the white and brown sugars, milk, pecans and butter. Bring to a rolling boil and boil for 1½ minutes (no longer). Remove from fire and add vanilla, then beat until creamy. Drop by spoonfuls on wax paper.

Mrs. J. P. Pfieffer
Bastrop, Texas

AUNT NEALE'S PEANUT BRITTLE

Pinch of salt
½ cup sugar
½ cup water
½ cup light corn syrup
1 cup raw peanuts
1 scant teaspoon baking soda

Mix salt, sugar, water and syrup, and cook until a drop makes a soft ball when dropped in water. Add peanuts and cook until they are done. They will begin to pop open. Drop a bit in water to see if candy is brittle. Add baking soda and stir well. Place on greased aluminum foil or sheet of wax paper. When cool, break into desired pieces.

Gladys Holmes
Houston, Texas

PEOPLE PUPPY CHOW

1 cup creamy peanut butter
2 cups chocolate bits
1 stick margarine
1 box Crispix cereal
Powdered sugar

Melt and pour over one box of Crispix cereal. Mix well. Shake by cupfuls in a bag of powdered sugar. Add more sugar as needed.

Hilma Nelson
Bastrop, Texas

SPICED SUGARED PECANS

1 cup granulated sugar
½ teaspoon ground cinnamon
⅓ cup evaporated milk
1 teaspoon vanilla extract
2 cups pecan halves

In a large saucepan, bring to a boil the sugar, cinnamon and milk. Stir constantly with a wooden or slotted spoon until mixture reaches soft-ball stage or until it begins to harden on sides of saucepan. Add vanilla and mix well. Remove from heat and add pecan halves.

Stir in pecans quickly, coating well with syrup mixture. Drop on sheet of wax paper and, as soon as pecans are cool enough, separate and let them cool thoroughly. These freeze very well for future use. Makes approximately 2½ cups.

Eloise Moore
Houston, Texas

COOKIES

BUTTER-PECAN SLICES

1 cup butter (use only butter)
2 cups brown sugar
2 eggs
1½ teaspoons vanilla
3½ cups flour
¼ teaspoon salt
1 teaspoon soda
1 cup chopped pecans

Blend butter, sugar, eggs and vanilla. Add sifted dry ingredients. Add nuts. Shape dough into a roll and place in refrigerator overnight. Slice thin and bake at 350° until golden brown.

Sandy LeBlanc
Rosenberg, Texas

BUTTER-SCOTCH COOKIES

1 cup shortening
1 pound light brown sugar
3 large eggs
1 tablespoon vanilla extract
3½ cups sifted flour
1 teaspoon salt
3½ teaspoons baking powder
1 cup chopped pecans

Cream shortening with sugar. Add eggs 1 at a time, beating well with mixer on medium. Add vanilla; mix well. Add flour, salt, baking powder and pecans, mixing all ingredients well.

Make 3 long rolls of dough, wrapping each roll in wax paper; refrigerate overnight. Slice rolls and bake cookies on greased cookie sheet at 350° about 15 minutes or until done.

You may also freeze the rolls of dough and bake them as needed. These cookies will keep indefinitely in a closed container after they are baked.

Variation: For Christmas, add red and green candied cherries, cut fine, to the cookie dough.

Louis Kowis
Livingston, Texas

PEANUT BUTTER COOKIES

½ cup peanut butter (chunky preferred)
¼ cup shortening
½ cup brown sugar
½ cup granulated sugar
1 egg
1 cup flour
1 teaspoon soda

Cream peanut butter and shortening together. Add sugars gradually. Beat until light and fluffy. Add egg. Stir well. Add flour and soda, and mix well. Form into little round balls and place on greased cookie sheet about an inch or 2 apart. Press down with tines of a fork—one way, then across. Bake 10 to 15 minutes at 350°. Wonderful!

Bill Springer
Producer
The Eyes of Texas

HONEY COOKIES

"My great-grandparents August and Caroline Weiss operated the first cotton gin operated by steam, near Salem in Washington County. They were among the first German settler in that area. Money was scarce; however, they always had bees and native pecans . . . consequently, this recipe was a favorite."

1½ pints honey, warmed
1½ cups brown sugar
Dash of salt
½ teaspoon cinnamon
1 cup chopped pecans or other nuts
1 teaspoon baking powder
Enough flour for very stiff dough

Mix all ingredients well. Roll dough out on a floured board and cut with a cookie cutter, or drop the dough in a greased pan and flatten with a floured glass. Bake at 325° until golden brown with edges slightly darker. These cookies will be somewhat chewy.

Ben Scholl
Tomball, Texas

TEXAS FRUIT-CAKE COOKIES

2 pounds dates
2 cups pecans
8 ounces candied cherries
8 ounces candied pineapple
2½ cups sifted flour
1 teaspoon baking soda
1 teaspoon salt
1 teaspoon cinnamon
1 cup butter
1½ cups sugar
2 eggs

Coarsely chop fruit and nuts. Sift flour, soda, salt and cinnamon together. Scatter some over fruit and nuts. Cream butter; add sugar, mixing until light and fluffy. Beat in eggs. To the creamed mixture add fruit, nuts and remaining dry ingredients. Mix well.

Drop by teaspoonfuls onto ungreased cookie sheet. Bake at 350° for 10 minutes. Remove from oven and cool. Makes about 125 cookies that keep well for several weeks.

Pat Farris Cummins
Bellaire, Texas

COCOONS

1 cup butter
4 tablespoons powdered sugar
Pinch of salt
2 cups chopped pecans
3 scant cups flour
2 teaspoons vanilla
Powdered sugar

Cream butter, sugar and salt. Add pecans. Mix in flour and vanilla. Form into balls and then shape like cocoons. Bake 40 minutes in a 275° oven. While cookies are hot, drop them in a bowl of powdered sugar.

Roy D. Plaisance
Angleton, Texas

CHOCOLATE LASSIES

¾ cup shortening
¾ cup brown sugar
1 egg, unbeaten
½ cup molasses
2½ cups sifted flour
1½ teaspoons soda
½ teaspoon ginger
½ teaspoon cinnamon
2½ cups chocolate chips
½ cup chopped nuts

Cream shortening and sugar until fluffy. Beat in egg and molasses. Sift flour, soda and spices. Add to shortening and mix well. Stir in chocolate chips and nuts. Bake at 375° 10 to 12 minutes. Makes about 4 dozen cookies.

Edith Hopkins
Wimberley, Texas

TEXAS COOKIES

2½ cups sifted flour
1 teaspoon baking powder
½ teaspoon salt
¾ cup butter or margarine, softened
¾ cup sugar
2 tablespoons milk
1 egg
1 teaspoon vanilla
1 cup oats (quick or old-fashioned)
1 cup finely chopped pecans

Sift flour, baking powder and salt into a bowl. Add butter, sugar, milk, egg and vanilla. Mix until well blended. Stir in oats and nuts. Roll out on lightly floured canvas to ¼-inch thick. Cut in Texas shape with Texas cookie cutter. Bake on greased cookie sheet at 375° for 15 minutes. Decorate with powdered sugar icing.

Lydia Spies
Houston, Texas

COWBOY COOKIES I

1 cup shortening
1 cup sugar
1 cup brown sugar
2 eggs
1 teaspoon vanilla
½ teaspoon salt
1 teaspoon soda
½ teaspoon baking powder
1 cup nuts
6 ounces chocolate chips
2 cups rolled oats

Blend shortening and sugars. Add eggs and vanilla, beating until light and fluffy. Add sifted dry ingredients and mix well. Add remaining ingredients. Drop onto greased cookie sheet and bake at 325° for 15 minutes. Makes 4 to 5 dozen.

Cassie Crowson
Alvin, Texas

COWBOY COOKIES II

1 stick margarine
3 tablespoons cocoa
2 cups sugar
½ cup milk
⅛ teaspoon salt
8 tablespoons peanut butter
3 cups quick oats
1 teaspoon vanilla

Mix first 5 ingredients in saucepan and bring to a rolling boil. Boil for 1 minute. Remove from heat and add peanut butter, oats and vanilla. Mix well and drop on wax paper. Cool for about 20 minutes.

Patricia Buckley
Friendswood, Texas

GRAMMA'S CHOCOLATE CHIP COOKIES

2 cups white sugar
2 cups brown sugar
1 cup butter or margarine
1 cup shortening
4 eggs
3 cups flour
2 teaspoons baking soda
2 teaspoons salt
3 cups oats (old-fashioned oats make a crunchier cookie)
2 cups Rice Krispies
2 teaspoons vanilla
1 large package chocolate chips

"Makes a lot for hungry kids."

Cream the first 4 ingredients. Add remaining ingredients, stirring carefully until well blended. If cookie batter is too thin, add a little flour. Bake at 350° until light brown and still a bit soft.

Judy McCleary
Houston, Texas

CHOCOLATE OATMEAL COOKIES

⅔ pound raisins
1 cup fig or strawberry preserves
1½ cups pecans
2 tablespoons rum
2 jiggers wine
1¾ sticks margarine, melted
2 cups sugar
4 eggs
4 cups flour
4 tablespoons cocoa
1¾ teaspoons salt
1¾ teaspoons baking soda
3½ teaspoons baking powder
¾ teaspoon ground cloves
1½ teaspoons cinnamon
1 cup buttermilk
4 cups rolled oats

"This recipe is an original of my grandmother's and yields 'the best cookies in the world!' My grandmother was Flora Bassett Thomas, a native of Gainesville, Texas, who lived her entire life in Texas."

The day before baking, grind or chop the first 3 ingredients and marinate overnight in rum and wine.

Mix margarine, sugar and eggs with mixer in a large bowl. Sift together flour, cocoa, salt, baking soda, baking powder and spices. Add to margarine mixture, alternating a little of the dry mixture with a little buttermilk until completely mixed (will resemble thick cake batter). Add oats and pre-prepared mixture of raisins, etc. Combine thoroughly. Mixture should be very stiff. Add more oats if necessary.

Drop by teaspoonfuls on greased cookie sheet. Bake at 325° for about 12 minutes or until firm to touch. After cooling, store between sheets of wax paper in a covered container. Cookies are even better the second day. Makes about 6 dozen small cookies.

Carolyn McCaine Damron
Austin, Texas

MAMA'S OATMEAL COOKIES

3 cups oatmeal
2 cups flour
1 cup sugar
1 tablespoon cinnamon
1 teaspoon soda
⅓ teaspoon salt
2 eggs, beaten
5 tablespoons milk
1 cup melted butter or margarine
½ cup chopped pecans and ½ cup raisins (optional)

Recipe of Nella Frances McAteer, born 1867; submitted by her great-granddaughter.

Mix all dry ingredients. Add eggs, then milk, then butter, mixing after each addition. Add nuts and raisins, if desired. Drop by spoonfuls onto ungreased cookie sheet and bake at 325° until lightly browned.

Frances Denton
Spicewood, Texas

COLD COFFEE COOKIES

2 cups brown sugar
1 cup butter
1 cup cold coffee
2 eggs
1 teaspoon soda
3 cups sifted flour
1 teaspoon nutmeg
1 teaspoon cinnamon
2 cups seedless raisins

Mix all ingredients together and drop by teaspoonfuls onto buttered pans. Bake at 350° for 12 to 15 minutes.

Dortha Altman
Conroe, Texas

PERSIMMON COOKIES

½ cup shortening
1 cup sugar
1 egg
2 cups flour
1 teaspoon soda
½ teaspoon cinnamon
½ teaspoon cloves
½ teaspoon nutmeg
1 cup persimmon pulp
1 cup raisins
1 cup nuts

"Submitted in memory of Eloise Sessum of Livingston, Texas."

Cream shortening and sugar. Add egg and beat well. Sift flour, soda and spices together and add alternately with persimmon pulp, beginning with flour. Add raisins and nuts. Drop onto greased cookie sheet 2 inches apart. Bake at 350° until golden brown.

Jessie Holifield
Splendora, Texas

TEXAS STARS

COOKIE DOUGH:
1⅓ cups flour
1½ teaspoons baking powder
¼ cup butter
¼ cup sugar
1½ teaspoons vanilla extract
⅛ teaspoon salt
1 unbeaten egg

FILLING:
¾ cup finely chopped pecans
⅓ cup sugar
Dash of salt
1 tablespoon melted butter
2 tablespoons water
⅛ teaspoon vanilla extract

Prepare filling by combining all 6 ingredients and mixing well; set aside.

To prepare cookie dough, begin by sifting flour and baking powder together; set aside. Cream butter and sugar well; add vanilla, salt and egg. Gradually add the dry ingredients, mixing well.

Roll dough out on floured board to ⅛-inch thickness. Cut out cookies with star-shaped cutter. Place a teaspoonful of the filling in the center of each star. Now bring the points upright; starting at the base, pinch sides together so points will remain upright, allowing filling to show. Place on ungreased cookie sheets.

Bake at 400° for 8 to 10 minutes. Allow to cool completely; store in airtight container.

Linda Faulk Strickland
Houston, Texas

SNICKER-DOODLES

½ cup shortening
½ cup butter
1½ cups sugar
2 eggs
2¾ cups flour
2 teaspoons cream of tartar
1 teaspoon soda
¼ teaspoon salt
2 tablespoons sugar
2 tablespoons cinnamon

Cream shortening and butter with sugar. Beat in eggs. Sift in combined dry ingredients. Roll dough in balls the size of a walnut. Dip in a mixture of 2 tablespoons sugar and 2 tablespoons cinnamon. Place on ungreased cookie sheet. Bake at 400° for 8 to 10 minutes. Makes about 3½ dozen.

Megan Lee McClung
Garland, Texas

CRACKLY GINGERSNAPS

¾ cup soft margarine
1 cup brown sugar, packed
¼ cup molasses or cane syrup
1 egg
2¼ cups flour
1¼ teaspoons baking soda
1 teaspoon cinnamon
1 teaspoon ginger
¼ teaspoon cloves
¼ teaspoon salt
Granulated sugar

"These are always part of the cookies that we bake for the Christmas season."

Cream margarine and sugar. Add molasses and egg, beating well. Sift together the flour, soda, spices and salt. Stir into the creamed mixture; cover and chill. Roll dough into balls the size of a small walnut. Dip each ball half-way into a dish of water, then into granulated sugar. Place sugared side up on a greased baking sheet 3 to 4 inches apart. Bake at 350° for 10 to 12 minutes. Remove from cookie sheet and cool on racks. Store in an airtight container. Makes about 4 dozen.

The sugar makes a crackly top when baked. The cookies are supposed to spread as they bake. If they don't, use less flour next time.

Jeannette Werner
Santa Fe, Texas

HARDTACK

1 cup brown sugar
2 eggs
1 cup chopped nuts
1 cup chopped dates
1 teaspoon baking powder
½ cup flour
Pinch of salt
Powdered sugar

Stir all together well, put in a greased pan, and bake at 350° until golden brown. Cut into squares and roll in powdered sugar while hot.

Harriett Glasscock
Houston, Texas

CHOCOLATE CARAMEL LAYER SQUARE

⅔ cup evaporated milk, divided
1 14-ounce bag of caramels
1 18½-ounce package German chocolate cake mix
¾ cup margarine
1 cup chopped pecans
1 6-ounce package chocolate chips

Put ⅓ cup milk with caramels in top of double boiler and melt, stirring constantly. Mixture may also be melted in a microwave. Blend cake mix, ⅓ cup milk and margarine with electric mixer until dough holds together. Stir in nuts. Put half of cake mixture into greased 9 × 13-inch pan. Bake at 350° for 6 to 8 minutes. Remove from oven and sprinkle chocolate chips over the crust. Then spread caramel mixture on. Crumble rest of cake mixture over the chips and caramel. Return to oven and bake another 20 to 30 minutes. Cool in pan. Then chill in refrigerator for at least 20 minutes before cutting into squares. Makes 3 dozen.

Debbie Kahanek
Lake Jackson, Texas

CHOCOLATE MERINGUES

1 cup butter or margarine
½ cup brown sugar
½ cup granulated sugar
3 egg yolks
1 tablespoon cold milk
1 tablespoon vanilla
2 cups sifted flour
¼ teaspoon salt
¼ teaspoon soda
1 6-ounce package semisweet chocolate pieces

Soften butter and cream with brown and granulated sugars. Add egg yolks and beat well. Add milk and vanilla alternately with sifted dry ingredients. Spread evenly in a well-greased 11 × 16-inch pan. Sprinkle with chocolate pieces. Set aside and prepare meringue topping.

MERINGUE TOPPING:
3 egg whites
1 cup brown sugar
1 cup chopped pecans

Beat egg whites until stiff; add brown sugar gradually. Fold in chopped pecans carefully. Spread over mixture in pan and bake at 350° for 25 minutes. Cool before cutting.

Yvonne Sartor
Baytown, Texas

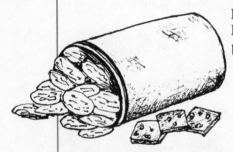

LILY KING'S SUGAR COOKIES

1 cup butter
1 cup sugar
1 egg
1 teaspoon vanilla
2 cups sifted flour
½ teaspoon soda
½ teaspoon cream of tartar

Cream the butter, sugar, egg and vanilla. Add sifted dry ingredients. Mix well and roll out dough on a floured board to about a ¼-inch thickness, and cut with a cookie cutter.

Sprinkle cookie dough with sugar and bake at 375° for 12 to 15 minutes.

Jean King Sitterle
Houston, Texas

WHITE BROWNIES

1 package white cake mix
1/3 cup brown sugar
1/3 cup milk
1 egg
1 tablespoon light corn syrup
1 cup chopped pecans
Red and green Hershey-ettes candies

Mix the white cake mix and brown sugar thoroughly. Combine milk, egg and corn syrup, then add to the cake mix. Stir in the pecans. Spread batter in an oblong pan, and add Hershey-ettes, arranging them in rows. Bake at 350° for 20 minutes, cool, and cut into bars.

Note: Hershey-ettes are sold only during the Christmas season. At other times, omit candies or substitute another kind.

Dorothy Ann Rothermel
Brenham, Texas

ROCKY ROAD BROWNIES

6 tablespoons butter
1 square unsweetened chocolate
1 cup sugar
1 teaspoon vanilla
2 eggs
3/4 cup flour
1/2 teaspoon salt
1/2 teaspoon baking powder
1/2 cup chopped pecans or walnuts
26 large marshmallows, cut in half

"I won a blue ribbon for this recipe at the County Fair."

In saucepan melt butter and chocolate over low heat; stir constantly. Remove from heat. Add sugar and vanilla; mix well. Beat in eggs. Stir together flour, salt and baking powder; add to chocolate mixture, blending well. Stir in nuts. Spread in greased 11 × 7-inch baking pan. Bake at 350° for 20 to 25 minutes. When done, immediately arrange marshmallows over top. Drizzle glaze around marshmallows.

GLAZE:
1 square unsweetened chocolate
1 tablespoon butter or margarine
1 cup powdered sugar
½ teaspoon vanilla
2 tablespoons hot water

Melt chocolate and butter over low heat; stirring constantly. Remove from heat. Stir in powdered sugar and vanilla until crumbly. Blend in hot water until of pouring consistency.

After drizzling glaze over top of brownies, return to oven for 2 to 3 minutes to melt marshmallows. Swirl with knife for a marble look. Cool. Cut with wet knife.

Janet Hronek
Somerville, Texas

BROWNIES

½ pound butter
4 squares of bitter chocolate
4 eggs
2 cups sugar
1¼ cups flour
2 cups pecans
1 tablespoon vanilla

Melt butter and chocolate in top of a double boiler. Mix well the eggs, sugar, flour and nuts. Add the butter, chocolate and vanilla to egg mixture. Bake in shallow pan about 25 to 30 minutes at 350°.

ICING:
½ box powdered sugar
Pinch of salt
½ square melted chocolate
2 tablespoons butter
Enough coffee to make mixture spread

Mix all ingredients well and spread on brownies while they are still warm.

"This came from the Whitehead Ranch in Del Rio to the J. B. Goodson Ranch about forty years ago."

Shotsie Dean
Magnolia, Texas

EDITH NURNBERG'S JAM SQUARES

"This is my mother's recipe for special cookies that she baked for my brother, sister, and me (and now for her grandchildren) when we were growing up. They are particularly tasty on cold nights, around exam time, and on any occasion that calls for sweet celebration. Jam Squares equal nurturing."

1⅔ cups all-purpose flour
½ cup light brown sugar, firmly packed
½ teaspoon salt
1 heaping teaspoon shortening
¼ pound sweet butter
2 eggs, at room temperature, separated
1 teaspoon vanilla extract
½ cup raspberry jam or preserves
½ cup sugar
¼ teaspoon cinnamon
¾ cup chopped walnuts

Combine flour, brown sugar and salt. Cut in shortening and butter. Beat egg yolks with vanilla, and add to dry ingredients. Mix in with hands. Press into ungreased 8 × 12 × ¼-inch pan. Bake for 15 minutes at 375°. When slightly cool, spread with jam. Beat egg whites until fluffy, gradually adding sugar and cinnamon. Spread on top of jam and sprinkle with walnuts. Bake at 375° for 20 minutes. Cut into squares while still hot in the pan. May be frozen and stored.

Ruth Nurnberg
Houston, Texas

CHERRY-CHEESE BARS

1 cup walnuts, divided in half
1¼ cups flour
½ cup brown sugar
½ cup shortening
½ cup coconut
1 8-ounce package cream cheese
⅓ cup sugar
1 egg
1 teaspoon vanilla extract
1 can cherry pie filling

Chop ½ cup walnuts coarsely for topping. Set aside. Chop remaining walnuts fine. Combine flour and brown sugar, cut in shortening until fine, then add nuts and coconut. Mix and remove ½ cup. Press remaining mixture into greased pan. Bake 12 to 15 minutes at 350°.

To make a filling, beat cream cheese, sugar, egg and vanilla until smooth. Spread over hot crust, return to oven, and bake 10 minutes longer. Spread cherry pie filling on cheese layer. Combine coarsely chopped nuts with crumb mixture and sprinkle onto cherry topping. Bake 15 minutes. Cool and cut into squares. For Christmas, sprinkle on a few green cherries.

Judy Fallin
Conroe, Texas

FRESH APPLE BARS

⅔ cup shortening
2 cups brown sugar
2 eggs, beaten
1 teaspoon vanilla
¼ teaspoon salt
2 cups sifted flour
2 teaspoons baking powder
1½ cups chopped raw apples
½ cup chopped nuts

Cream shortening and sugar. Add eggs, vanilla and salt. Beat well. Sift flour and baking powder, and add to mixture gradually. Stir in apples and nuts.

Bake in greased 12 × 12 × 3-inch pan at 350° for 35 to 40 minutes. Cut into bars when cool.

Mrs. Salvador Brown
Dickinson, Texas

MOTHER'S APPLE CRISP

8 apples, peeled and sliced
½ cup sugar
½ teaspoon cinnamon
½ teaspoon nutmeg
½ cup water
1 teaspoon lemon juice
1 cup sugar
¾ cup flour
½ cup softened butter or margarine

Place apple slices in bottom of large baking dish. Combine in a small bowl ½ cup sugar, cinnamon and nutmeg. Sprinkle on top of apples. Combine water and lemon juice and pour over apples. Combine 1 cup sugar, flour and butter, and crumble over apple mixture. Bake 30 minutes at 350°. May be served warm with a scoop of vanilla ice cream.

Margaret Nelson
Baytown, Texas

APPLE CRISP

3 or 4 medium apples
¾ cup quick-cooking oats
½ cup flour
¾ cup brown sugar
1 teaspoon cinnamon
¼ cup butter

Pare apples and slice thin. Arrange in greased baking pan. Mix oats, flour, brown sugar and cinnamon. Cut in butter. Sprinkle over sliced apples. Bake at 350° for 35 to 40 minutes.

Lenee MacDonald
Romayor, Texas

INDEX

NOTES:

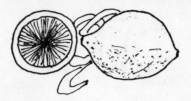

NOTES:

NOTES: